FORMULA FOR SUCCESS
IN LIFE, CAREER AND BUSINESS

FORMULA FOR SUCCESS

IN LIFE, CAREER AND BUSINESS

PETER STEELE

Think! Plan! Take Action! Never Quit! Succeed!

Published by Peter Steele
petersteele1378@gmail.com

First published 2020
Reprinted 2025

© 2020 Peter Steele

The moral right of the author has been asserted.

All rights reserved.
Without limiting the rights under copyright restricted above, no part of this publication may be reproduced, stored in or introduced into a retrieval system, or transmitted, in any form or by any means (electronic, mechanical, photocopying, recording or otherwise), without the prior written permission of the copyright owner and publisher of this book.

Disclaimer: This book has been written to provide the reader with a general guide on achieving success. The advice and strategies may not be suitable to satisfy every situation nor to satisfy the needs of every person. It is sold on the understanding that the author and the publisher and each of them separately shall not be liable or responsible in any way to any person or legal entity with respect to any loss or damage directly or indirectly suffered by that person or entity as a result of the information provided in this book.

 A catalogue record for this book is available from the National Library of Australia

ISBN 978 0 6450244 1 8 (pbk)
ISBN 978 0 6450244 2 5 (ebk)

Designed and typeset by Helen Christie, Blue Wren Books
Cover photos by Keyur Nandaniya on Unsplash
Logo designed by Noreen Pratap
Printed by Ingram Spark

To my wife Teena, with love

CONTENTS

About the Author ix
Foreword xi
Preface xiii
Acknowledgements xv

INTRODUCTION 1

DIVISION 1: THE FORMULA
    1. Your Primary Goal 7
    2. Your Obstacles 17
    3. Your Opportunities 29
    4. Your Special Knowledge 45
    5. Your Plan 57

DIVISION 2: THE WINNER'S MINDSET
    6. A Sufficient Winner's Mindset 77
    7. Your Essential Strengths 95
    8. Your Driving Strengths 107
    9. Your Supportive Strengths 119
    10. Your Attributes, Traits and Good Health 133
    11. Your Weaknesses 149
    12. Acquiring Your Sufficient Winner's Mindset ... 163

DIVISION 3: SELF ANALYSES AND REALITY CHECKS
    13. Your Self Analyses 177
    14. Your Reality Checks 187

IN FINAL CONCLUSION 199

Think! Learn! Take Action! Never Quit! Succeed!

ABOUT THE AUTHOR

The author, Peter Steele, has been described as a modern day Napoleon Hill.

He practiced law, both as a barrister and a solicitor for many years in Australia and overseas, but is now retired from the legal profession.

His book helps people of all ages from widely differing background from around the world to attain success in life, career and business and to successfully achieve their goals.

He has considerable experience as a public speaker, having spoken in Australia and other countries at seminars and other events primarily in relation to success and wealth creation through property investment. He has also conducted various live courses on wealth creation through investment in residential real estate.

He is passionate about helping others attain a high level of success.

It is for this reason that he has written this book — *Formula for Success in Life, Career and Business.*

FOREWORD

I met Peter Steele in 1969 when we worked as criminal lawyers in Papua New Guinea, then a territory of Australia. We have maintained contact since then notwithstanding that our respective career paths diverged, mine as a barrister in Queensland and the Northern Territory of Australia and his as a successful commercial lawyer. It is as a commercial lawyer that Peter learned from his many clients singularity of purpose and the need to succeed. From one particularly tenacious and very hard working client he came to understand a formula for success which, with Steele adaptations, forms the basis of this book.

Peter is focused and passionate about his subject and I get the distinct impression that this book is also a testament to that particular client. Peter is correct to describe the subject as timeless but in this book his personal experience necessarily backgrounds his words. The formula exposed in this book provides a much needed guide to the successful and practical achievement of success in life, career and business.

While the achievement of success in life, career and business has been documented by others, this book's unique contribution is that it explains in readily understandable language the way to achieve that success. The book is in two parts. The first part deals with the creation of a written plan identifying the goal or objective to be achieved and the principles or guidelines underpinning the achievement of that goal or objective. The second part explains how to achieve the written plan involving as it does the need for singularity of purpose and positive character strengths and attributes. The appendices at the end of the book involving self analysis and reality check questions are effectively associated with the second part of the book.

The book is written in a conversational style which is easy to read and easy to understand. Its benefit over other books on success is that it is clearly based on much practical experience and knowledge of what is actually required to achieve success. It is much more than a statement of platitudinal desires. The deliberative process involved in the achievement of one's stated goal is what Peter calls "The Formula for Success in Life, Career and Business".

This book represents an important contribution to an important subject. Notwithstanding its importance in life, career and business, little if any attention is given to the subject in our schools and tertiary institutions. This book is more than capable of filling that gap. Readers will profit from the techniques involved in achieving success which are explained in the book. Achieving success involves more than merely desiring it. What is required is clearly explained in this book. I have no doubt that if properly applied the formula will enable readers to achieve success in whatever they set out to do.

Clive Wall RFD, QC

Judge, District Court of Queensland 1996-2016.
Judge, Planning and Environment Court, Queensland 1996-2016.
Air Commodore, RAAF.
Deputy Judge — Advocate General, Australian Defence Force 2006-2008.

PREFACE

Have you ever thought about what it would be like to develop the ability to achieve every material goal that you set yourself in life, career, business or whatever else you set yourself to achieve?

It would be life changing.

Formula for Success in Life, Career and Business will teach you how.

You must simply read, learn, understand and properly apply the information contained in this book and keep applying it until you succeed.

That's your challenge. No one will do it for you. You must do it for yourself.

When you do — not "if" but "when" — you will ensure yourself success in your endeavours.

This book has been written by the Author to provide a practical guideline on how to achieve success and create wealth.

Properly apply the information that this book provides, never quitting until you succeed. Doing so will provide you with a life-long path to success and abundance.

Welcome to *Formula for Success in Life, Career and Business*.

ACKNOWLEDGEMENTS

In my opinion, Napoleon Hill is the forefather of modern literature dealing with success and wealth creation and I acknowledge him as such. In particular I acknowledge the great contribution that his books The *Law of Success* and *Think and Grow Rich* have made in those fields.

Whilst I may not agree with all his ideas, I agree with and endorse many of them. I have adopted and re-written some of his ideas in my own words and combined them with my own. In doing so I have formulated the set of principles that constitute the *Formula for Success in Life, Career and Business*.

I have sought to distil the information in a clear, concise manner and to present the book in an instructional format.

Many of the fundamental ideas and concepts expressed in this book and by Napoleon Hill are timeless.

And, I acknowledge and thank my former client and friend, Tan Sri Loy, now sadly deceased.

Tan Sri was born in Malaysia of Chinese parents. He started his business life in his teens, selling fuel to passing motorists from two forty-four gallon drums at the roadside near a rubber plantation in Malaysia. From those humble beginnings, he built a successful multi-million dollar international business in finance, property and trading.

I spent many hours discussing the subject of success with Tan Sri. The principles he applied in life and business to attain his remarkable success are, for the most part, set out in this book.

INTRODUCTION

The information contained in *Formula for Success in Life, Career and Business* has the power to enable you to be highly successful in life, career and business and help you attain every goal that you set yourself.

By learning, understanding and properly applying the information provided in this book, you stand to gain extraordinarily positive results in whatever you set out to achieve.

In essence, the principles underlying the successful attainment of your every goal may be summarised as follows:

- You must firstly know what it is that you wish to achieve and precisely define it in writing, leaving no uncertainty as to your intended goal;
- You must identify the various obstacles that stand in your way, hindering or preventing you from attaining your intended goal;
- You must identify the various opportunities available to you or which you must create and use in order to overcome your obstacles;
- You must identify and acquire the special knowledge which you must have or which would be helpful in assisting you to attain your goal;
- You must formulate a written plan which details how you will use your opportunities to overcome your obstacles, how you will acquire the special knowledge identified and, where

reasonably possible, your plan should include the time limit in which you propose to achieve your goal;
- You must work your plan with dedicated singularity of purpose, never quitting until you successfully accomplish your goal — one step at a time .

Whilst it's relatively simple to formulate and write a plan, it's far more difficult to work it day-by-day, week-by-week, month-by-month, year-by-year, never quitting until you successfully attain your goal.

For that, you must have a powerful unrelenting mindset — a winner's mindset that is sufficient to keep you driven and to never quit until you succeed. It is the most powerful and important element of achieving success.

Once you truly acquire a sufficient winner's mindset and learn and properly apply the information provided in this book, you'll be in a very strong position from which to achieve your every goal and attain the highest level of success.

Every idea that you have is a product of your mind. Every goal that you set starts with an idea, whether you conceive the idea or obtain it from others.

In life, career and business, opportunities will come to you. They may be generally available on the market, they may be specifically offered to you or you may create them. When opportunity knocks, recognise and assess it. If it's what you want, seize and work it, never quitting until you fully develop and use it to your full advantage.

It takes careful planning, hard work and a sufficient winner's mindset to bring your every opportunity to a successful fruition.

Dedication, commitment and hard work are a must, but never underestimate the importance of also maintaining good physical and mental health. Good health and physical and mental well being often prove essential. You must have the physical and mental capacity that may prove necessary in order to successfully attain your goal.

You are probably reading this book, because you are searching for a pathway that will lead you to success.

Search no further. You have found it.

Whether you should follow through, learn and properly apply the information provided in this book depends upon whether you are ready to receive and apply it. Don't waste your time until you are. Ensure that you are ready, not only to receive the knowledge and the guidelines, but also to commence taking whatever action is necessary and to follow through, never quitting, until you successfully achieve your goal.

How do you ascertain if you are ready?

First ask yourself if you are truly serious about being a successful person in everything you choose to do?

If your answer is affirmative, ask yourself the second question.

"Am I truly prepared to do whatever is necessary, always in a strictly ethical manner and to immediately and relentlessly pursue my goal without procrastination, to the exclusion of all other goals, until I successfully achieve it?"

If you again answer in the affirmative to all parts of the second question and really mean it, you are ready to embrace the teachings of this book and use them in order to attain the highest level of success in your life, career and business and to successfully pursue your every goal.

So let's get on with it. Let's just do it!

Welcome to *Formula for Success in Life, Career and Business* and the best of success to you!

DIVISION 1
THE FORMULA

1
YOUR PRIMARY GOAL

Fundamental Principle One
Identify and precisely define your primary goal in writing.

You need to know precisely what you want to achieve as your primary goal because it's only when you know precisely what you want that you will be in a position to plan precisely what you must do to achieve it.

What is your primary goal?

It is your most important goal. It is the one goal that, at this particular time in your life, you most want to achieve; more than any other goal.

It must be a material goal that is measurable. It must be a goal that is entirely under your control to achieve. It cannot be a goal that involves, for example, love, emotional attachment or some similar desire that requires another person to reciprocate your feelings. Whether, or not, the other person is of the same mind as you, is a matter that is under the control of that person. You cannot force another to feel the same way as you do. You may certainly try and you may certainly set yourself those types of goals, however, they are not goals that will necessarily be achieved using *Formula for Success in Life, Career and Business*. The formula provided in this book is only concerned with the achievement of material goals that are under your control to achieve. Of course, you may obtain the assistance of others to help you attain your goal providing you retain control and guide the outcome.

Your task is to select the one goal that is your most important goal at this particular time in your life and pursue it to the exclusion of all other goals. This does not mean that you may only have one primary goal during your lifetime. You may have several. Most people do. However, it means that you must pursue only one primary goal at any one time. Every other goal becomes a secondary goal. After you have achieved your primary goal, you may then precisely define your next primary goal and pursue it to a successful conclusion in the manner shown in this book.

By pursuing more than one goal at a time, you distract yourself. In so doing, you destroy your singularity of purpose and, as a result, you substantially diminish your chances of success.

Identify and define your primary goal

The process for identifying and selecting your primary goal is to take the time to think carefully about every goal in your bucket list that you would like to achieve and make a written list of every one of them as they come to mind. From that list, select three goals that you consider are your three most important. Delete all the other goals you have written down. From your list of three, you must then select the one goal that you absolutely know is your most important.

The one goal that you finally select as your most important at that particular time in your life, is your primary goal.

Write down your primary goal, using as many words as you wish to generally describe it. Every goal starts as an idea or thought in your mind. By writing it down, you have taken what's in your mind and committed it to paper. In doing so, you have taken the first step in turning your thoughts into reality. You have taken the first step towards achieving your primary goal.

Your next step is to take what you have written as a general description of your primary goal and rewrite it with such accuracy that you know precisely what it is, leaving no doubt, setting out exactly what it is and, where possible, the date by which or the time period within which you want to achieve it.

For example, suppose that you wish to travel to a city in order to visit a friend at his or her home and you write a travel plan for your journey. Obviously if you wish to visit your friend at home, you must know the address. It is an essential part of your travel plan. If it only states that your destination is Sydney, London, New York or whichever other city you are visiting, it is not sufficiently precise. If you simply commit the address to memory, but forget it, you'll have a problem when you arrive in the city, especially if for some reason, you are unable to contact your friend. If your written travel plan has been sufficiently detailed and you have included all necessary information such as your friend's address, you will have no problem. You cannot readily achieve a specific goal unless it is precisely defined in writing. Having it in writing provides you with a permanent record that you may refer to at any time.

At this stage, also give some thought to the time period you will reasonably require in which to achieve your primary goal. Understand that if your primary goal is one that will take some time to achieve, it may not be possible, at this early stage, to state with accuracy the date by which or the time within which you will achieve it. The reason is that there may be various factors, not properly known to you at the time of making your estimate, which may affect the time period needed to achieve your goal. Unforeseen circumstances may arise that cause delay. Certainly, put pressure on yourself to achieve it within your specified time, but always consider whether the time period you have allowed yourself is reasonable, given all your circumstances. Those circumstances (if any) that are likely to affect your time period will become clearer while you are working through your plan to achieve your goal.

Using another example, suppose you have a plan to take a holiday with your family. You estimate the cost of the holiday at $5,000 and your plan includes saving $500 per month until you have the required amount. All is going well, until unforeseen circumstances arise which result in you losing your job. You have no alternative other than to put your holiday plan on hold until you find employment and are able to reassess and resume your savings plan at a level that will depend on your future earnings. In those circumstances you will need to reassess the time period in which you will be able to save the money needed for your holiday. Your circumstances may, and often will, change as a result of factors beyond your control, so it's difficult to accurately assess the time period that you will need in order to achieve your goal. Changing circumstances may leave you with no alternative, other than to adjust your time period.

Whatever is necessary in order to achieve your primary goal and the time period within which to achieve it will depend, to a large extent, upon your personal circumstances at the time that you set your primary goal and the circumstances beyond your control, if any, that arise during the period you attempt to achieve it.

In all cases, where time is not of the essence, always remember it's more important to achieve your goal than to achieve it within a particular time.

As part of this chapter and each of the next four chapters you will be asked to complete an exercise. Apart from their instructional value, the five exercises have a practical purpose because when you have completed them, your answers will have completed each step necessary to achieve your primary goal including details of how you will achieve it.

Exercise 1 is set out at the end of this chapter. In it, you are asked to identify and clearly and concisely define your primary goal in writing.

Five examples to assist you to complete Exercise 1

In order to assist you to properly complete Exercise 1, please consider the five different examples set out in this chapter. The examples show how those persons cited in the examples have completed their answers to Exercise 1 and, in so doing, have identified and defined their respective primary goals.

Example 1

A young man has a dream to buy a home within the next five years.

The facts relating to him are:
1. He is employed as a real estate salesperson earning a retainer of $500 per week and, on average, a sales commission of $1,000 per week.
2. Over the last three years, he has achieved an average gross income (based on his retainer and his sales commission) of $78,000 per annum.
3. He has no savings.

He takes into consideration what he wants to achieve and completes his Exercise 1 by identifying and defining his primary goal as follows:

Within the next five years, I will purchase a three bedroom property on the Gold Coast in Queensland as my home for a purchase price of $400,000.

Example 2

An overweight middle-aged lady has been talking about losing weight for years and has finally decided to do something about it.

The facts relating to her are:
1. She is married with three children. She is a full time housewife who is supported by her husband.
2. Her husband earns a slightly below average weekly wage, the majority of which is spent on paying the rent and supporting his wife and family. There is very little, if any, surplus cash left at the end of each week.
3. She is forty-eight kilograms heavier than the weight that is considered a healthy weight for a person of her age and height.
4. She is concerned about the adverse affect that her obesity is having on her mobility and health.

She takes into consideration what she wants to achieve and completes her Exercise 1 by identifying and defining her primary goal as follows:

Within one year, I will lose forty-eight kilograms in weight and thereafter continue to maintain a healthy weight for my age and height.

Example 3

A young girl, who has recently completed her secondary education, wishes to obtain a degree in veterinary science in order to follow her dream career as a veterinary surgeon.

1: Your Primary Goal

The facts relating to her are:
1. She is in her late teens and lives at home with her parents who support her.
2. She lives in Sydney, Australia and has recently completed her secondary education. Her dream is to study for her degree at Sydney University.

She takes into consideration what she wants to achieve and completes her Exercise 1 by identifying and defining her primary goal as follows:

Within the next six years, I will obtain a veterinary science degree from Sydney University to enable me to practice as a veterinary surgeon.

Example 4

A man in his thirties has decided to quit smoking.

The facts relating to him are:
1. He is an excellent tennis player who plays competitive tennis for his club. Excelling in his sport is one of his passions.
2. During the last few months while playing tennis, he has been suffering severe shortage of breath and is concerned that it is adversely affecting his performance on the court.
3. He realises that his shortage of breath directly results from the fact that he is a smoker.

He assesses his condition and believes that unless he stops smoking, his ability to play tennis at his best will continue to deteriorate.

He takes into consideration his desire to do whatever is necessary to excel at tennis and to remain sufficiently fit to do so and completes his Exercise 1 by identifying and defining his primary goal as follows:

I will quit smoking immediately and never smoke again.

Example 5

A husband and wife are business partners and operate a successful accountancy practice. They wish to double the current gross annual income of $1,500,000 earned by their practice, increasing it to $3,000,000 per annum.

The facts relating to them are:
1. They are both qualified chartered accountants.
2. Their practice currently has an annual gross turnover of $1,500,000 per annum. By earning an additional $1,500,000, they will double their practice's income and earn a gross annual income of $3,000,000.
3. They enjoy an excellent reputation as chartered accountants.

They believe they have the ability to substantially increase their clientele and to double their gross income.

They take into consideration what they want to achieve and complete their Exercise 1 by identifying and defining their primary goal as follows:

Within the next three years we will increase the gross income earned by our accountancy practice to a minimum of $3,000,000 per annum and we will, at least, maintain it at that minimum level each year thereafter.

EXERCISE 1
To identify and define your primary goal

Like everything you conceive, your goal starts in your mind as an idea or thought. At this early stage it is most probably not fully identified and not precisely defined.

In this Exercise you are asked to identify and precisely define your primary goal in writing.

Before completing Exercise 1, please read and understand the five examples in this chapter. They should assist you to better formulate and define your primary goal when completing your exercise.

Your guidelines for completing this Exercise are:
1. Firstly write down every goal that you would like to achieve in general terms using as many words as you wish. The easiest way is to write down a bucket list of everything you'd like to do or achieve. Take your time and ensure that you write down every goal that comes to mind. Read them through several times, think about them carefully and select the three goals from your bucket list that you consider to be the three that you would most like to achieve.
2. Now, scrap all the other goals and repeat that process with the three goals that you have selected and from those three, select the one goal that you are absolutely certain is your most important goal — the one that you'd most like to achieve.
   Your final selection is your primary goal.
3. Think about it. Think about exactly what you want to achieve and describe your primary goal generally, using as many words as you wish to describe it.
4. Now condense and summarise what you have written, using the following guidelines:
   a) State precisely what you want to achieve;
   b) Be short, concise and absolutely specific — try and keep it to around 50 words or less;
   c) Leave no doubt, uncertainty or ambiguity; and
   d) As part of your summary, include the date by which or the time within which you intend to achieve your goal.

When you are satisfied with the final written draft of your answer to Exercise 1, please write or type it on a blank sheet of A4 paper under the heading "My Primary Goal".

In conclusion

At the end of Exercise 1, you will have completed a vital step in the process. You will have identified your primary goal.

You will have taken your general idea and precisely defined it in writing and, in doing so, you will have extracted it from your mind and clearly and precisely committed it to paper.

Once it is clearly defined, you will know precisely what you must achieve. There can be no ambiguity. Your goal must be completely unambiguous as you move forward to achieve it.

Your answer to Exercise 1 constitutes the first part of your 'blueprint' for achieving success.

File your written answer to Exercise 1 in a folder entitled: "Achieving My Primary Goal". Keep the folder in a safe place, ensuring you have easy and immediate access to it at all times.

As you complete each Exercise, you will be asked to file the final draft of your answer for each Exercise in the same folder. When you have completed all your Exercises, the folder will contain the step-by-step written guide, including your plan of what you must do to attain your primary goal.

2
YOUR OBSTACLES

> **Fundamental Principle Two**
> Identify and define in writing the material and mindset obstacles that stand between you and the achievement of your primary goal.

What are your obstacles?

They are the obstacles that stand between you and the achievement of your primary goal. They may be divided into two categories, namely:
- Your material obstacles; and
- Your mindset obstacles.

Your material obstacles are those obstacles that have physical or material form or substance such as 'lack of cash' or 'lack of physical fitness'.

If your goal is to acquire a house, a car, a yacht, an overseas trip or other item and you do not have the cash to do so, your major obstacle is a lack of cash equivalent to the purchase price of the particular item that you wish to acquire. Similarly, if your goal is to set up a business and you lack the capital, your major obstacle is the lack of capital you need to invest in the business.

If on the other hand, your goal is to run a full marathon and win the event, cash is probably not an obstacle unless, of course, you don't have the cash for the entry fee. Your major obstacle in this case, is to prevent yourself from being beaten across the finish line by the other competitors in the race.

You may encounter several material obstacles when attempting to achieve your primary goal. They will depend on your particular goal, your particular circumstances and any circumstances, beyond your control, that may arise. Lack of cash is probably the one that is most frequently encountered but there are many others — lack of qualifications, a bad credit rating and debilitating ill health, to name a few.

Your mindset obstacles are caused by your particular mindset. An example of a mindset obstacle is a 'lack of willpower'. Who you are as a person is to a large extent governed by what and how you think. Your character is a product of your mind. It affects who you are, what you say and how you say it, how you react to other people and how you react to the pressures of life, career, business or anything else. Having control over your mind is an essential ingredient in controlling the outcome of everything you do and say and, to a large extent, what you achieve.

Some of us are more reluctant to admit our shortcomings than others. If you deny your shortcomings you are deluding yourself. Now is not the time to be in denial. If you are, this denial is in itself a mindset obstacle that stands between you and the achievement of your goal.

Identifying your mindset obstacles is highly important. However, identifying them is often more difficult than identifying your material obstacles. To a large extent, identifying your mindset obstacles is a matter of self-analysis. This requires you to be brutally honest with yourself and admit your defects. You cannot overcome a mindset obstacle unless you recognise and admit that you lack the particular mindset quality needed, such as a lack of determination, a lack of commitment, a lack of persistence or whatever else it may be.

Identify and define your obstacles

At this stage you are only concerned with identifying the material obstacles and the mindset obstacles that stand in your way. You are not currently concerned with how you will overcome them. The next chapter deals with identifying those opportunities that are immediately available to you and those that you need to create in order to overcome both your material and mindset obstacles.

When you identify your material and mindset obstacles, only identify those that exist at the time you make your identification. Do no pre-empt what obstacles may arise in the future. You may update your lists of obstacles at a later stage if circumstances change.

Later chapters of this book provide you with information on a number of character strengths, attributes and traits. When you read them, you may discover that you lack one or more of them. If so, you may discover that the lack of those strengths, attributes or traits constitute mindset obstacles that you did not consider when initially identifying them. When you complete Exercise 2 at the end of this chapter, your answers will identify and define those mindset obstacles known to you at the time of completing the Exercise. Filing and keeping your answers will enable you to revisit and update your answers from time to time in the future if you identify new mindset obstacles as a result of changing circumstances and knowledge that you gain about yourself.

In order to plan how you will attain your primary goal you must firstly identify the obstacles that are blocking you from achieving it. Once you know precisely what those obstacles are, you will then be in a position to formulate and prepare a plan on how you will overcome them.

Exercise 2 is set out at the end of this chapter. In it, you are asked to identify and define each of the material and mindset obstacles that stand in your way, preventing you from achieving your primary goal.

Five examples to assist you to complete Exercise 2

As with the previous chapter, you have been provided with the same five examples, except that those examples are now advanced to the next stage to ascertain how the persons referred to in them have respectively answered their Exercise 2 and identified their respective obstacles. The examples should assist you to properly complete your Exercise 2.

Example 1

A young man has a dream to buy a home within the next five years.

Further facts relating to him are:
1. He has calculated that the cash he needs to purchase his home in the present market is an amount of $420,000 including the purchase price of $400,000 and an estimated sum of $20,000 to cover stamp duties, legal, finance and other associated costs.
2. He currently has no cash in the bank and no other immediate access to any of the cash needed.
3. He understands that over the next five years the cost of purchasing his desired house will most probably increase. If this occurs, he will need to make the appropriate adjustments to his purchase price and other cash requirements.
4. He recognises that he tends to live for today. He is overly generous and spends all his surplus cash every week and has no savings plan.

5. He also recognises that he frequently changes his mind and focus on what he wants to achieve.

He takes into consideration his calculations and character traits and completes his Exercise 2 by listing his obstacles as follows:
1. *The material obstacles that I face are:*
   a) *I do not have the $420,000 or any part thereof that I need to purchase my house.*
   b) *The sum of $420,000 needed on today's market will probably increase over the next five years.*
2. *The mindset obstacles that I face are:*
   a) *My tendency to overspend.*
   b) *My total lack of commitment to a savings plan.*
   c) *My general lack of persistence.*

Example 2

An overweight middle-aged lady has been talking about losing weight for years and has finally decided to do something about it.

Further facts relating to her are:
1. She eats a lot of junk food and drinks a lot of soft drink.
2. She eats between meals every day and often gets up at night to eat chocolates, biscuits or cake and washes them down with soft drink.
3. She eats an excessive amount during meals.
4. She never exercises.
5. She has a tendency to be lazy and lacks willpower, always putting off until tomorrow what needs to be done today.
6. She thinks that her easiest way to lose weight will be to join a weight loss program, buy diet meals, join a gymnasium and engage a personal trainer to help her with an exercise regime.

She takes into consideration her financial situation, bad habits and laziness and completes her Exercise 2 by listing her obstacles as follows:
1. *The material obstacles that I face are:*
   a) *The lack of money necessary for me to join a weight loss program and buy the diet meals I need from the weight loss company.*
   b) *The lack of money I need to join a fitness club and pay a personal trainer to put me through the fitness program I need.*
2. *The mindset obstacles I face are my lack of persistence and willpower.*

Example 3

A young girl, who has recently completed her secondary education, wishes to obtain a degree in veterinary science in order to follow her dream career as a veterinary surgeon.

Further facts relating to her are:
1. Her matriculation grades were not high enough for her to gain admission to study her desired degree at Sydney University.
2. She is a singularly determined young lady. When she sets her mind on something, she seldom quits until she achieves what she wants.
3. She lacks the money to pay her university fees, to buy the books she will need and to support herself during her studies.

She takes into consideration what she wants to achieve and completes her Exercise 2 by listing her obstacles as follows:
1. *The material obstacles that I face are:*
   a) *My lack of a sufficiently high matriculation grade to gain admission to Sydney University to study for my desired degree in veterinary science.*
   b) *The lack of funds necessary to pay my university fees, to buy the books I need for my studies and to support myself during my studies.*

c) When I do gain admission, which I will, the necessity to pass my exams and gain my degree.
2. I consider that I have no mindset obstacles that will prevent me from achieving my goal.

Example 4

A man in his thirties has decided to quit smoking.

Further facts relating to him are:
1. He has a well-paid job but is under constant pressure to achieve results. He suffers extreme anxiety and stress as a result of his job. He tends to smoke heavily in the mistaken belief that it helps him to relax and that it de-stresses him.
2. Although a relatively determined person, he has not succeeded in quitting smoking despite several previous attempts.

He takes what's necessary for him to give up smoking into consideration, the adverse affect that smoking is having on his tennis and completes his Exercise 2 by listing his obstacles as follows:
1. *I do not face any material obstacles.*
2. *The only mindset obstacle that I face is my lack of willpower.*

Example 5

A husband and wife are business partners and operate a successful accountancy practice. They wish to double the current gross annual income of $1,500,000 earned by their practice, increasing it to $3,000,000 per annum.

Further facts relating to them are:
1. They both wish to retire. Their plan is to double the gross income of their accountancy practice in order to increase its goodwill and so increase its sale price. They have determined

that with a gross annual income of $3,000,000, the sale price of their practice will be sufficient to enable them to retire.
2. They propose to acquire several new clients and to progressively engage a sufficient number of qualified accountants to handle the additional work.
3. In order to achieve their goal they have calculated that they will need to invest a capital sum of $100,000. This sum will be required to progressively employ up to three new accountants, with around $30,000 per accountant being needed to pay their initial wages and other costs until they each earn sufficient fees to cover their respective salaries and other outgoings.
4. Their accountancy practice is well established and has been profitable since its establishment. They are both set in their ways and having to double their client base will require a new direction that will take them outside their comfort zone.

They take into consideration their calculations and assessments and complete Exercise 2 by listing their obstacles as follows:
1. *The material obstacles that we face are:*
   a) The possible lack of the sum of $100,000 at the time when it will be required for business expansion.
   b) The lack of a sufficient client base from which to earn an additional income of $1,500,000 per annum.
   c) The lack of a sufficient number of competent qualified chartered accountants to handle the additional work that will be generated by our new clients.
2. *The mindset obstacles we face are the possible lack of determination, persistence and resolve to successfully achieve our planned expansion.*

EXERCISE 2
To identify and define your obstacles

This Exercise requires you to identify and precisely define your material obstacles and your mindset obstacles under separate lists.

You are asked to identify and then precisely define firstly the material obstacles and then the mindset obstacles that you consider stand in your way preventing you from achieving your primary goal.

Please read and understand the information provided in this chapter including the five examples as many times as you may need. When satisfied that you have a full understanding of the information you need and what is expected of you, please complete Exercise 2.

After you have identified and properly defined them, you will know precisely what material and mindset obstacles you believe you must overcome in order to achieve your primary goal. In order to overcome them, you must firstly determine and understand what they are.

Your guidelines for completing this Exercise to identify and define your material obstacles are:

1. Firstly, think carefully about every material obstacle that you consider may be a material obstacle that stands between you and the achievement of your primary goal.
2. As they come to mind, write each of them down, making a list of your material obstacles on a sheet of A4 paper headed "My Material Obstacles". Ensure that you list every material obstacle that comes to mind.
3. Think carefully about every material obstacle that you have listed and describe them generally in writing, using as many words as you need to convey a general description of them.

4. Once you have generally described each of them in writing, re-write each of your descriptions as clearly and concisely as you are able, using as few words as you consider necessary to convey a precise, but full description of each material obstacle.

Your guidelines for completing the second part of this Exercise to identify and define your mindset obstacles are the same as those provided for your material obstacles. It is the same process. For the mindset obstacles, prepare a separate list on A4 paper headed "My Mindset Obstacles".

On completion of Exercise 2, you will have identified and precisely defined in writing every material and mindset obstacle known to you at that time and which stands between you and the attainment of your primary goal.

When satisfied with the final written draft of your lists and the condensed descriptions of your material and mindset obstacles, they are the answers to your Exercise 2.

There is of course nothing to prevent you from expanding those lists with further items in the future, if you discover further material or mindset obstacles.

In conclusion

At the end of Exercise 2, you will have completed the next vital step on your pathway to success by identifying and defining your material and mindset obstacles. Once they are clearly defined, you will know precisely what stands in your way, preventing you from achieving your primary goal.

Your answers to this Exercise 2 constitute the second part of your 'blueprint' for achieving success.

File your written answers to Exercise 2 in your folder entitled "Achieving My Primary Goal".

As you complete each Exercise, your folder will grow until it finally contains your completed written plan. At this stage it will contain the second step that you must take to attain your primary goal.

3
YOUR OPPORTUNITIES

Fundamental Principle Three
Identify and define the material and mindset opportunities that you possess and create and define those that you need but do not possess.

What are your opportunities?

They are the opportunities that provide you with the means to overcome the obstacles that stand in your way, preventing you from achieving your primary goal. They may be divided into two categories, namely:
- Your material opportunities; and
- Your mindset opportunities.

Your material opportunities are those opportunities that are either immediately available to you or which you are able to create and utilise in order to overcome your material obstacles.

If a material opportunity is not available to you to use in order to overcome a material obstacle, you must find or create that opportunity.

If, as stated in the previous lesson, the material obstacle preventing you from acquiring a house, a car, a yacht, an overseas trip or other item is the lack of cash needed to purchase it, then you must ask yourself how you will obtain the necessary cash. In other words what avenues are open to you through which to obtain the necessary cash? Those avenues are your material opportunities. There are various material opportunities that may be immediately available to you. The most apparent is that you may apply to your bank or a finance company for the required funds. If your bank is prepared to lend you, say 80% of the funds required, it will be necessary for you to find the 20% shortfall. If you do not have the shortfall and cannot obtain it from another source, you must create the means through which you will acquire it. For example you could open a savings account and regularly bank part of your earnings into the account until you save the cash equivalent of the 20% needed.

In effect, you would have identified the bank as your material opportunity through which to borrow 80% of the money you require. You would have also created a material opportunity through which to obtain the balance of the funds needed by regularly setting aside part of your earnings.

Using another example, suppose your primary goal is to abseil off the top of a tall building. You will not be permitted to do so unless you firstly obtain permission from the owner or building manager. That is your first obstacle. You must search and find an owner or building manager prepared to give you permission to abseil off their building. Without that permission, you do not have the opportunity. You need to use your imagination and initiative to find the owner or building manager of a tall building that is suitable for your purpose and obtain the necessary permission. By doing so, you will have created your material opportunity. How you obtain the necessary permission is a matter for your ingenuity. Perhaps you could obtain permission by using the event to raise funds for a worthwhile charity.

Material opportunity is all around you. It may or may not always be obvious. When a material opportunity is not immediately apparent, search for it. Always use your imagination and initiative to create your material opportunity whenever and wherever possible. When you recognise a material opportunity, seize it and use it to your advantage.

Never underestimate the power of opportunity or the importance of seizing and using every opportunity that presents itself to you. Imagination is the tool that unlocks the door to opportunity and is especially powerful when coupled with an ability to 'think outside the square'.

The first place to look for material opportunity is at your feet. It's often right there in front of you. It's simply a question of recognising it.

There is an old saying that the grass is greener on the other side of the hill. It's not always true. It often seems to be greener — in your mind. It's good to always be looking for greener pastures, because it usually means that you are looking for new or better opportunities. But, it's not good to always be looking for opportunities over the hill if all you are doing is pandering to the whims of a restless mindset.

Always be aware that greener pastures may not be over the hill and may not be what they seem. They may be at your feet. It may be that you have simply not recognised them. They may be found in your job or your business. You may not yet realise the material opportunities that your job or business holds for you. When you find opportunity, remember to use your imagination and initiative to enhance it wherever possible. Every material opportunity may hold the seed to your success.

Don't go charging over the hill looking for those greener pastures, before you stop and carefully look around you. The place to start searching for opportunities is right there in front of you.

The time to start searching for material opportunities is right now. Never procrastinate.

Whenever action is needed, take it immediately.

Your mindset opportunities are those opportunities that are available to you or are attainable by you in order to enable you to acquire the character strengths, attributes and traits that will enable you to overcome your mindset obstacles. They will give you that singularity of purpose and never quit attitude that will intensify your persistence and keep you on track until you succeed.

Previously we used the example of a person who wished to run and win a marathon. One of the challenges of competing in a marathon is the physical challenge of attaining the high degree of physical fitness necessary to enable you run and compete in the race at the peak of your performance level. It could take many years. Miles and miles of running and training, day after day, week after week and month after month of every year in order to gain that level of physical fitness. Unless you have the persistence and the willpower to drive yourself to do the training, you will never become a top-level marathon runner.

The mindset obstacles that will prevent you from becoming a top-level marathon runner and from winning your marathon event could be the lack of persistence, willpower or both. The mindset opportunities that you need to overcome them are the opportunities to develop or strengthen and maintain the necessary strengths of persistence and willpower.

You must acquire all those mindset strengths, attributes and traits that you do not possess and for those that you do not possess at a sufficient level, you must develop and strengthen them. In other words, you must acquire a sufficient winner's mindset to overcome all your mindset obstacles.

Your opportunity to do so is contained in this book. It provides you with the information and know how necessary to do so.

Identify and define your opportunities

The process for identifying and recognising your opportunities are essentially the same as those you used to identify and recognise your obstacles. As with your obstacles, you are only concerned with identifying and defining those opportunities.

When you identify your material and mindset opportunities, identify only those that you will need to overcome the material and mindset obstacles that you have identified and defined at that particular time.

If, after completing later chapters of this book, you discover that you may have missed certain mindset obstacles, you may then re-visit the matter and identify and update those mindset opportunities required to overcome your newly identified mindset obstacles.

As part of your plan to attain your primary goal, you must identify and define every opportunity you will need to help you to overcome each and every obstacle that is blocking you from achieving it. The opportunities may already exist and be readily available to you. If not, you must create them.

Visualise and think carefully about your every material and mindset obstacle and every material and mindset opportunity that is needed to overcome them — the opportunities that exist and those that you must create.

Exercise 3 is set out at the end of this chapter. In it you are asked to identify and define each of the material and mindset opportunities that you will need in order to respectively overcome the material and mindset obstacles that stand in your way, preventing you from achieving your primary goal.

Five examples to assist you to complete Exercise 3

As with the previous chapter, you have been provided with the same five examples, except that those examples are now advanced to the next stage to ascertain how the persons in those examples respectively completed their Exercise 3 to identify and define their particular material and mindset opportunities.

Example 1

A young man has a dream to buy a home within the next five years.

Further facts relating to him are:
1. He enjoys his job. He has good prospects of advancing to a management position. He does not wish to lose the security provided to him by his job.
2. His sole source of income is derived from his job.
3. He works five days per week from Monday to Friday except on public holidays.
4. He has a good credit rating.
5. His bank manager has advised him that under the bank's serviceability criteria (having regard to his annual gross income) for a property that values at $400,000, he could borrow $320,000 from the bank to purchase it. He was also advised that the bank would seek to secure the loan by taking a first mortgage over the property and that the loan amount would not exceed 80% of the bank's valuation of the property.
6. He needs $420,000 in cash. He has calculated that if he borrows $320,000 from the bank his shortfall will be $100,000 providing that the property is not valued at less than the purchase price. Spread over five years he believes he is capable

of acquiring the shortfall at an average savings rate of $20,000 per annum net after tax.
7. On average he currently makes 24 sales per annum. He believes that by hard work, he has the ability and the opportunity to double his current sales rate. If so, he will also receive a significant annual incentive bonus from his employer. The bonus coupled with his retainer and sales commissions will result in increased earnings in excess of $20,000 per annum net after tax. It will also increase his borrowing capacity from the bank.
8. He has purchased a copy of this book.

After taking into consideration his circumstances, he decides that all the material opportunity he needs to purchase a home at a cost of $420,000 is available to him through his bank, his job, his projected earnings and proposed savings plan.

He has read this book and believes that it provides him with the opportunity to acquire a sufficient winner's mindset and that once acquired, it will assist him to overcome all his perceived mindset obstacles including his propensity to overspend, his inability to save money and his lack of persistence.

He completes his Exercise 3 as follows:
1. *The material opportunities available to me to overcome my material obstacles are:*
   a) *To borrow the sum of $320,000 from my bank; and*
   b) *To earn an additional amount of $20,000 per annum net after tax for the next 5 years by doubling the number of sales I make at work each year."*
2. *I have read* Formula for Success in Life, Career and Business *and it provides me with the opportunity to acquire the character strengths, attributes and traits I need to overcome my mindset obstacles. When I acquire a sufficient winner's mindset, I will have everything necessary to ensure that I work persistently to achieve*

my increased sales targets and to save my additional income until I have the $100,000 I need.

Example 2

An overweight middle-aged lady has been talking about losing weight for years and has finally decided to do something about it.

Further facts relating to her are:
1. She has decided that she cannot afford to join a weight loss program or buy diet food through the program or to join a gymnasium or engage a personal trainer unless she gets a job or starts a business from home to earn the extra money.
2. She does not wish to get a job or start a business. She realises that she has alternative opportunities.
3. Alternatively, if she stops eating junk food and drinking large quantities of soft drink and regulates her eating habits, she will lose weight. Further the only exercise she needs is to start walking every day, increasing the distance she walks and the speed at which she walks, as she loses weight and her condition improves.
4. Her alternative material opportunities require no cash and, by cutting out junk food, soft drinks and excessive eating, she will save money and, as a result, have more cash available to her for necessities.
5. She has purchased a copy of this book.

After taking into consideration her circumstances and considering her alternatives she completes her Exercise 3 as follows:
1. *I do not require any material opportunities other than the diet and exercise programs that I shall create.*
2. *I have read* Formula for Success in Life, Career and Business *and it provides me with the ability to access the mindset opportunities I need to overcome my mindset obstacles. When I acquire a sufficient*

winner's mindset, it will give me the willpower that I need to exercise and regulate my diet.

Example 3

A young girl, who has recently completed her secondary education, wishes to obtain a degree in veterinary science in order to follow her dream career as a veterinary surgeon.

Further facts relating to her are:
1. After investigation, she has discovered that she may gain admission to study for a veterinary science degree at Sydney University by repeating her matriculation year. However admission will still depend on whether she gains the necessary matriculation grade on her second attempt.
2. She has also discovered an alternative way of gaining admission. She already has the matriculation grade necessary to gain immediate admission to study at Sydney University for a degree in veterinary nursing and that after successfully completing part of that degree, she will be entitled to gain admission by transferring from studying for a veterinary nursing degree to studying for a veterinary science degree.
3. She has decided upon the alternative course of action and will seize the opportunity to gain admission to Sydney University to study for a degree in veterinary science by firstly gaining admission to study for a degree in veterinary nursing and partly completing that degree to the necessary extent.
4. Further investigation has revealed that she is eligible to enrol in the HECS-Help scheme under which the Commonwealth Government of Australia will pay her university and tuition fees, repayable by her in instalments after she graduates and starts working.
5. She will avoid accommodation costs by continuing to live at home and her parents have offered to provide her with the

money to cover her living costs and to purchase the textbooks needed for her course.
6. Her parents have recently purchased this book and given it to her as a present.

After taking into consideration her circumstances and considering her alternatives she completes her Exercise 3 as follows:

1. *The material opportunities available to me to overcome my material obstacles are:*
   a) *To gain admission as a student to study for my veterinary science degree by firstly gaining admission to Sydney University to study for a degree in veterinary nursing and partly complete that degree to the extent required before transferring and studying for my veterinary science degree.*
   b) *To enrol in the HECS–Help scheme under which the Australian government will pay my university fees and allow me to repay them by making periodic deductions from my wages after I have graduated and am working.*
   c) *To live free of charge at home with my parents and accept their offer to pay my living expenses and to buy the textbooks I will need.*
2. *Whilst I consider that I do not require any mindset opportunities to overcome mindset obstacles for the purpose of gaining admission to Sydney University and completing my degree in veterinary science, I have read* Formula for Success in Life, Career and Business *and know that if I ever need to do so, I may use the information provided in the book to acquire a sufficient winner's mindset. It will substantially reinforce my resolve and stand me in good stead in assisting me to achieve my goal.*

Example 4

A man in his thirties has decided to quit smoking.

Further facts relating to him are:

1. He realises that he has suffered several temporary setbacks in his previous attempts to quit smoking.
2. He has looked at the reasons for his temporary setbacks and concluded that he has never been fully committed to quit smoking. He has found alibis and made excuses all through his previous attempts. He deluded himself into the mistaken belief that by attempting to reduce the number of cigarettes each day, he was working his way towards finally quitting. He talked a lot about quitting but never took the final step.
3. He believes his recent difficulties of breathing while playing tennis has given him a real desire to quit smoking and that he is now fully committed to do so.
4. He now believes that the only "sure fire" way to quit smoking is to stop "cold turkey" and never smoke again.
5. He has purchased a copy of this book.

He assesses his situation and completes his Exercise 3 as follows:

1. *I do not require any further material opportunities.*
2. *I have a copy of* Formula for Success in Life, Career and Business *and the knowledge contained in the book provides me with all the mindset opportunities I need to overcome my mindset obstacles. When I acquire a sufficient winner's mindset, I will gain the willpower, determination and total commitment that I need to quit smoking, by simply stopping and never smoking again.*

Example 5

A husband and wife are business partners and operate a successful accountancy practice. They wish to double the current gross annual income of $1,500,000 earned by their practice, increasing it to $3,000,000 per annum.

Further facts relating to them are:
1. Discussion with their bank manager has revealed that their bank is prepared to provide them with a business loan to

cover the $100,000 required for business expansion in order for them to cover the wages of new employees and any other related costs.
2. The wife will devote herself full-time to running the practice and the husband will devote himself full-time to expanding the business by gaining new clients.
3. They have discussed the nature of the work the husband will now undertake and realise it will take him well outside his comfort level.
4. They have purchased a copy of this book.

They take into consideration all their circumstances and complete their Exercise 3 as follows:

1. *The material opportunities available to us to overcome our material obstacles are:*
   a) *To obtain a business loan of $100,000 from our bank and draw down on the loan, as required from time to time for any additional costs resulting from our expansion including any increase in wages.*
   b) *To recruit and hire additional chartered accountants, as required, by using an employment bureau that specialises in recruiting chartered accountants.*
   c) *To actively sell the services of the firm with a view to attracting suitable new clients requiring audit, tax and general accountancy services.*
2. *We have read* Formula for Success in Life, Career and Business. *The knowledge provided in the book will provide us with the mindset opportunities that will enable us to overcome any mindset obstacles that either of us have or may encounter. When each of us acquires a sufficient winner's mindset, it will give us the power to follow through and complete our respective tasks in order to expand our accountancy practice by acquiring new clients and to do whatever else proves necessary.*

EXERCISE 3
To identify and define your opportunities

This Exercise requires you to identify and precisely define your material and mindset opportunities under separate lists.

You are asked to identify and then precisely define firstly the material opportunities and then the mindset opportunities that will enable you to respectively overcome the material and mindset obstacles that stand in your way, preventing you from achieving your primary goal.

Please read and understand the information provided in this chapter including the five examples above, as many times as you may need. When satisfied that you have a full understanding of the information you need and what is expected of you, please complete Exercise 3.

After you have identified and properly defined them, you will know precisely what material and mindset opportunities you must possess in order to overcome your material and mindset obstacles. In order to use or create your opportunities, you must firstly determine and understand what they are.

Your guidelines for completing this Exercise to identify and define your material opportunities are:

1. Firstly, think carefully about every material opportunity that you consider is available to you, or which you must create, to provide you with the means to overcome every material obstacle that is preventing you from achieving your primary goal.
2. As they come to mind, write each of them down, making a list of your material opportunities on a sheet of A4 paper headed "My Material Opportunities".

Ensure that you list every material opportunity that comes to mind.
3. Think carefully about every material opportunity that you have listed and describe them generally in writing, using as many words as you need to convey your description of them.
4. Once you have generally described each of them in writing, rewrite them as clearly and concisely as you are able, using as few words as you consider necessary to convey a precise, but full description.

Your guidelines for completing the second part of this Exercise to identify and define your mindset opportunities are the same as those provided for your material opportunities. It is the same process. For the mindset opportunities prepare a separate list on A4 paper headed "My Mindset Opportunities".

On completion of Exercise 3, you will have identified and precisely defined in writing every material and mindset opportunity that you consider will be necessary to enable you to overcome the material and mindset obstacles that stand between you and the attainment of your primary goal.

When satisfied with the final written draft of your lists and condensed descriptions of your material and mindset opportunities, they are your answers to your Exercise 3.

There is of course nothing to prevent you from expanding that list with further items in the future, if you discover further material opportunities or mindset opportunities.

In conclusion

At the end of Exercise 3, you will have completed the next vital step on your pathway to success by identifying and defining your material and mindset opportunities. Once they are clearly defined, you will know precisely what opportunities you possess, need or must create in order to overcome your obstacles and assist you to achieve your primary goal.

Your answers to this Exercise 3, constitute the third part of your 'blueprint' for achieving success.

File your written answers in your folder entitled "Achieving My Primary Goal".

As you complete each Exercise, your folder will continue to grow. It now contains the third step that you must take to attain your goal.

4
YOUR SPECIAL KNOWLEDGE

> **Fundamental Principle Four**
> Identify and briefly define in writing the material and mindset special knowledge that you will need or that will be helpful in assisting you to achieve your primary goal.

What is special knowledge?

Special knowledge refers to the special knowledge, training and/or qualifications that you must have or is important to acquire in order to enable you to fully utilise your opportunities in pursuit of the successful achievement of your primary goal.

It may be divided into two categories:
- Your material special knowledge; and
- Your mindset special knowledge.

Whatever life, career, business or other path you decide to undertake, you must acquire the necessary material special knowledge that you will require in order to successfully undertake it. As the first step in that process, you must assess what material special knowledge, training or qualifications you will need, having regard to what you want to do.

In deciding what material special knowledge you require, you must consider the purpose for which you need it. In other words, what material special knowledge do you consider or know that you must have in order to achieve your particular primary goal?

The answer lies in what service, trade, profession, business or other life path or goal you wish to pursue. Once you know what you want to do, you'll then be in a position to know and ascertain what material special knowledge you will need.

For example, if you wish to be a lawyer, you will need to firstly acquire a law degree and then undergo such other courses as may be required to permit you to practise law as a profession at your intended location. If you wish to be a plumber, you will need to serve an apprenticeship and acquire the necessary qualifications. If you wish to be a real estate salesperson, you will, depending on local legal requirements, probably need to obtain a real estate salesperson's licence and in addition, you probably need sales training and product knowledge.

If achieving your primary goal involves others, such as your employees, you will need to ensure that they have the necessary material special knowledge, training and qualifications, depending upon what duties they are employed to carry out.

Never underestimate the material special knowledge that comes from experience. Never underestimate the importance of gaining the material special knowledge that can be gained from observing others or from taking advice from others with experience in the particular field in which you are engaged.

Whilst material special knowledge is often absolutely essential to your future success, it will not, in itself, bring you success. Material special knowledge is merely a necessity that will permit you to follow your chosen path or to follow it to better advantage or will assist you to do so. Success depends on how effectively you use your material special knowledge.

Never feel disadvantaged or in any way inferior if you have not completed a formal, secondary or other educational course. Depending upon what you want to achieve, completion of your secondary or other education is irrelevant unless it is a necessary prerequisite to obtaining a tertiary education or other qualification; for example, a prerequisite to gain admission to university. What is relevant is the material special knowledge you need for your specific purpose. Remember that many highly successful men and women never completed a secondary or other type of formal education

For those successful men and women, an unquenchable desire, total commitment, absolute determination, unwavering persistence and a never quit, never say die attitude were far more important. Many of them acquired their knowledge by self-education or by engaging the services of experts where needed.

It's never too late to learn. You can always learn something new. Keep your eyes and ears open. Be receptive to learning. Be receptive to new knowledge and ideas. Be especially receptive to new knowledge and ideas that help you gain the material special knowledge you need or is helpful.

In summary, you will acquire the material special knowledge you need:

- From formal education such as a university degree or a tertiary diploma;
- From specialised training, such as on the job training or other training courses;
- From your personal experience;
- From the experience of others who are engaged in the same field; and
- From research and self-education.

If you are at a stage in your life where you are acquiring a formal education whether at secondary school, or at a university or training college, your focus should be on successfully completing your chosen subjects at school or the successful acquisition of your university degree or college diploma, as the case may be. Similarly, the successful completion of any specialised training.

Once you have achieved your educational or training goal, you may then determine where that could potentially lead you and what doors it may open.

In addition to the material special knowledge that you will need in order to achieve your material goal, you will also need the mindset special knowledge that will enable you to acquire a sufficient winner's mindset.

If we return to the earlier reference to people who have attained great success in life without completing their secondary education, the common factor that distinguishes them is that they all possess an unquenchable desire, total commitment, absolute determination, unwavering persistence and a never quit, never say die attitude. They all possess a sufficient winner's mindset. For them, having the right mindset was the determining factor that enabled them to finally achieve success despite all the numerous temporary setbacks that they may have encountered along their path.

You may gain a sufficient winner's mindset by studying the relevant chapters in this book and applying the principles that you learn. *Formula for Success in Life, Career and Business* provides you with the special knowledge you need for that purpose. Whether you truly achieve a sufficient winner's mindset depends on whether you possess or develop the dedication and singularity of purpose to do so.

Identify and define the special knowledge you need

Recognising the material special knowledge that you require is relatively simple. It's simply a question of writing a list of the qualifications you consider you will need in order to enable you to achieve your primary goal. Too much detail is not required. For example, if you intend to pursue a career as a lawyer, you'll need a bachelor of laws degree from a recognised university and whatever subsequent qualifications that the body governing the practice of law as a profession at your intended location, requires. In turn, it may depend on whether you intend to practice as a barrister or solicitor.

In the case of a profession or trade, simply contact the governing body that regulates the particular profession or trade in the region that you wish to practice and ascertain the educational requirements, if any, that you need. Where specific material special knowledge is not a requisite, you may identify the material special knowledge that will benefit you and gain it from personal experience, by talking with others engaged in the same business or through self-education.

At this stage, your sole concern is to identify in writing the material special knowledge that you consider you will need. You should also identify in writing the mindset special knowledge that you consider that you will need to overcome those mindset obstacles that you have identified.

After you read this book, you will discover that it contains all the mindset special knowledge that you will require.

Exercise 4 is set out at the end of this chapter. In it you are asked to identify the material and mindset special knowledge that you consider you will need and that will help you.

Five examples to assist you to complete Exercise 4

As with the previous chapter, you have been provided with the same five examples, except that those examples are now advanced to the next stage to ascertain how the persons in those examples respectively answered their Exercise 4. The examples should assist you to properly complete your Exercise 4.

Example 1

A young man has a dream to buy a home within the next five years.

Further facts relating to him are:
1. He completed his secondary education and has a real estate sales person's licence.
2. He has had no formal sales training. He has learnt to sell by trial and error on the job.
3. He has access to information on the products he sells.

After thinking about his special knowledge needs he has answered Exercise 4 as follows:
1. *The material special knowledge I require is:*
    a) *Sales training, especially to improve my ability to properly make a sales presentation and successfully close the sale at the conclusion of the presentation; and*
    b) *A comprehensive knowledge of the real property I'm selling so that I may explain its capital growth potential and other financial benefits to prospective purchasers.*
2. *The mindset special knowledge I require is contained in* Formula for Success in Life, Career and Business. *By identifying, studying and applying that relevant information, I will acquire all the mindset special knowledge that I require.*

Example 2

An overweight middle-aged lady has been talking about losing weight for years and has finally decided to do something about it.

Further facts relating to her are:
1. She never completed her secondary education, but left school aged fifteen years of age and worked as a check out girl on a cash register at the local supermarket.
2. She fell pregnant at the age of seventeen and married the father of her child a month before the child was born. She has not worked since her marriage.

After thinking about her special knowledge needs, she has answered Exercise 4 as follows:
1. *The material special knowledge I require is to:*
   a) *Acquire more knowledge about weight loss diets; and*
   b) *Acquire knowledge about walking and other exercises in order to most effectively enable me to reduce weight and improve my level of fitness.*
2. *All the mindset special knowledge I need to successfully reach my goal is contained in* Formula for Success in Life, Career and Business. *I will read and study the information in the book and by doing so, I will acquire all the mindset special knowledge that I require.*

Example 3

A young girl, who has recently completed her secondary education, wishes to obtain a degree in veterinary science in order to follow her dream career as a veterinary surgeon.

Further facts relating to her are that she has now gained admission to study for a degree in veterinary nursing at Sydney University.

After thinking about her special knowledge needs she has answered Exercise 4 as follows:

1. *The material special knowledge I require is the knowledge I will be provided by Sydney University that will enable me to initially pass my exams whilst studying veterinary nursing and subsequently the knowledge I will need to pass my exams and obtain my veterinary science degree.*
2. *I do not consider that I require any mindset special knowledge, however all that special knowledge, if needed, is contained in* Formula for Success in Life, Career and Business *and if at any time I consider that I need it, I will obtain it from the book.*

Example 4

A man in his thirties has decided to quit smoking.

He has considered the fact that his sole obstacle is his lack of willpower to overcome his craving for nicotine. He already knows the heath hazards associated with smoking.

After thinking about his special knowledge needs, he has answered Exercise 4 as follows:

1. *I do not consider that I require any further material special knowledge.*
2. *I consider that all the mindset special knowledge I require is contained in* Formula for Success in Life, Career and Business. *I will read and study the book and use the information to acquire all the mindset special knowledge that I require in order to gain a sufficient winner's mindset.*

Example 5

A husband and wife are business partners and operate a successful accountancy practice. They wish to double the current gross annual income of $1,500,000 earned by their practice, increasing it to $3,000,000 per annum.

They have considered the fact that they lack experience in actively seeking out and acquiring new clients. Previously, they have not actively solicited clients, but simply allowed their practice to grow over the years through referrals and being approached by clients. They now recognise that if they intend to grow the practice as quickly as possible, they must actively seek to acquire new clients and this will take them outside their comfort zone. The husband, in particular, needs the knowledge that will enable him to attract and recruit new clients and sell them the services offered by their chartered accountancy practice.

He needs the mindset knowledge to overcome any reticence he might suffer as a result of operating outside his comfort zone.

After thinking about their special knowledge needs, they have answered Exercise 4 as follows:

1. *The material special knowledge he requires is the material special knowledge needed to effectively market and sell the accountancy services offered by the practice to new clients.*
2. *The mindset special knowledge that we respectively require is the knowledge required to ensure that we are able to engender the drive and persistence necessary to continually and consistently operate outside our comfort zone. All the knowledge we need in that regard is contained in* Formula for Success in Life, Career and Business. *We will read, study and apply the information in the book until we each acquire a sufficient winner's mindset to keep us on track.*

EXERCISE 4
To identify the special knowledge needed

This Exercise requires you to identify in writing the material and mindset special knowledge you consider that you will need.

You are asked to identify the special knowledge on separate lists, firstly all the material and then the mindset special knowledge that you will need in order to fully utilise your opportunities and successfully attain your primary goal.

Please read and understand the information provided in this chapter including the five examples as many times as you may need. When satisfied that you have a full understanding of the information needed and what is expected of you, please complete Exercise 4.

After you have identified the special knowledge, you will know what material and mindset special knowledge you will need. In order to acquire the knowledge, you must firstly determine and understand what it is and why you need to acquire it.

Your guidelines for completing this Exercise to identify your material special knowledge needs are:

1. Firstly, think carefully about the material special knowledge that you consider necessary or that will be a definite advantage in assisting you to achieve your primary goal.
2. Make a written list of your material special knowledge needs on a sheet of A4 paper headed "My Material Special Knowledge Needs". Ensure that you list all of them.
3. It is not necessary to describe the special knowledge if it is a formal degree, diploma or course, but simply to identify it by its title; for example, a law degree, a cooking diploma or a course in dress design. If it is not a formal qualification, you may describe it to the extent necessary to identify it.
4. Once you have completed your identification in writing, read and carefully check what you have written and ensure that your identification is clear, concise and accurate.

Your guidelines for completing the second part of this Exercise to identify your mindset special knowledge needs are similar. It's a process of identifying and listing all those strengths, attributes and traits that you consider you do not possess or that you do not possess to a sufficient level. They are your mindset special knowledge needs. List them on a sheet of A4 paper under the heading "My Mindset Special Knowledge Needs."

On completion of Exercise 4, you will have identified in writing the material and mindset special knowledge that you need or should acquire.

When satisfied with the final written draft of your two lists of your respective material and mindset special knowledge needs, they are the answers to your Exercise 4.

There is of course nothing to prevent you from expanding that list, with further items in the future, if you discover further special knowledge needs.

In conclusion

At the end of Exercise 4, you will have completed the next step on your pathway to success by identifying your material and mindset special knowledge requirements. Once they are clearly identified, you will know precisely what knowledge you will need in order to facilitate the achievement of your primary goal.

Your answers to this Exercise 4 constitute the fourth part of your 'blueprint' for achieving success.

File both lists containing your written answers in your folder entitled "Achieving My Primary Goal".

As you complete each Exercise, your folder has continued to grow. It now contains the fourth step that you must take to attain your primary goal.

5
YOUR PLAN

> **Fundamental Principle Five**
> Formulate and prepare a written plan through which to achieve your primary goal within a specified period of time.

What is your plan?

You have precisely defined your primary goal and you know exactly what you want to achieve. You have identified the obstacles that stand between you and the achievement of your primary goal. You have identified the opportunities that you will use to overcome your obstacles. And, you have identified the special knowledge that you must or should acquire to achieve your primary goal.

Whilst your primary goal is a material goal, the obstacles that you have identified as preventing you from achieving your goal, the opportunities that are available or that you must create and the special knowledge that you must or should acquire may relate to material and mindset matters.

Your plan is a written statement detailing how you will utilise or create and use your opportunities, step-by-step, until you overcome your obstacles, acquire your special knowledge and achieve your primary goal within your specified time period.

To the extent necessary, your plan must include all relevant material and mindset aspects.

You must formulate your plan in writing.

Your chances of achieving success in any endeavour in life, career, business or any other pursuit are greatly enhanced if you have a step-by-step written plan by which to achieve it. When it's a clearly defined written plan, you may refer to it as often as necessary to keep yourself on track, ticking each step as you achieve it and overcoming every obstacle that stands in your way. It is the action plan that moves you forward, step by step, until you overcome every obstacle and achieve every interim goal and target and finally your primary goal.

A written plan lays it out for you. It makes it certain. It plots precisely what you must do on a step-by-step basis, to achieve your primary goal. It's no longer a series of vague thoughts floating around in your mind. You now have a clear properly formulated course of action that, if doggedly followed without diversion or procrastination, will get you there. It's only a matter of time before you achieve your primary goal. It's your road map to success. Your plan will turn your wishes into reality, but only if you action it and never quit until you succeed.

More often than not, a primary goal is far too big to achieve immediately or within a short time. If so, you should follow the "Giant Watermelon Rule".

How do you eat a giant watermelon?

The answer is that you cut it into bite-size pieces and eat it piece by piece over a period of time until you have entirely consumed it.

The opportunity to eat the watermelon is right there in front of you. It is sitting there on your kitchen table ready to be eaten. It's just too big to eat in one sitting and will take several days to eat.

So, you work out a plan of how you will eat the watermelon and you follow the plan. You cut it into small bite size pieces, you select how many pieces you'll eat each day and, depending on your daily allocations, you may then accurately calculate how many days it will take you to eat it. That will be the time period you set yourself to achieve your goal.

You plan includes keeping the watermelon in a refrigerator or freezer to keep it fresh and systematically eat your daily allocations until you have eaten the lot. If you systematically follow your plan, eating your daily allocation each day, you will consume the watermelon within the time period you have allocated.

However, regardless of how well you plan, Murphy has a habit of popping up and thwarting you. The best laid plans of mice and men.

In this case, suppose it's the height of summer. The temperature has been over 40° centigrade for the last two days and the heat wave is expected to continue for the next couple of weeks. You have cut your huge watermelon and divided it into the daily portions. Based on your plan, you intend to consume those portions over a period of the next ten days.

You make room in your refrigerator and pack all you pieces of watermelon in bags in the refrigerator, together with a number of the bags in the freezer section.

Of course, that's when Murphy strikes. The refrigerator breaks down. You immediately arrange for a refrigerator technician to fix the problem. He comes to your home, identifies the problem and informs you that he will need to order and have a replacement part delivered. Without it, he cannot fix the fridge. He calls the local supplier and orders the spare part only to be informed that it will be at least two weeks before the part is available.

Meanwhile, the temperature of the interior of the refrigerator and its freezer section is steadily rising and you know that the watermelon pieces will not last the time period you have allocated.

Failure to consume the watermelon, for whatever reason, is not an option. You must make a contingency plan. You must do whatever is necessary. You cannot afford to buy a new fridge.

Instead, you use your large icebox to house the watermelon. You transfer your watermelon pieces into the icebox and pack it with ice. You will need to keep buying ice everyday to preserve your watermelon. And, that's what you do.

Quitting is not an option! You must do whatever is necessary. You must make such changes and such contingency plans as may prove necessary to enable you to successfully achieve your goal.

And so it is with achieving your primary goal or any interim goal or target. If they are too big, divide them into achievable pieces and achieve them piece by piece over an allocated period of time. If the time period you have allocated proves impractical, adjust it as required. And remember, if time is not of the essence, it's more important to achieve your goal or target than to achieve it within a particular time period. If problems arise, you must create whatever contingency plans are necessary to overcome them.

Formulate and identify your plan

Formulate your plan after careful consideration and write it down. Set out how you will systematically use you opportunities to overcome your obstacles and achieve your primary goal. Always do whatever is necessary. Quitting is never an option!

However at this early stage, your plan may not be formulated as precisely as it should be. Don't worry. Formulate your plan in general terms. When you start working your plan, you may discover interim goals and targets that need to be attained as part of the step-by-step process towards the final achievement of your primary goal. In these circumstances, amend your plan, fleshing it out to include those steps to achieve the interim goals and targets as part of your overall plan. Update and re-formulate your plan as often as needed.

Five examples to assist you to complete Exercise 5

As with the previous chapter, you have been provided with the same five examples, except that those examples are now advanced to the final stage to ascertain how the persons in those examples respectively completed their Exercise 5 to formulate their particular plans. The examples should assist you to properly complete your Exercise 5.

Example 1

A young man has a dream to buy a home within the next five years.

He has identified that his material obstacle is the lack of $420,000 and that his opportunities to acquire the money are to borrow $320,000 from his bank and earn and save an additional amount after tax of $100,000 over the next five years at an average net rate of $20,000 per annum.

He feels confident that with the right mindset, he is capable of earning the additional money at his job. He has decided that he will earn an additional $20,000 every year by increasing the number of sales he makes at work.

Further facts relating to him are:
1. He has calculated that he must double his sales rate to a total of forty-eight sales every year; an additional twenty-four sales per year. This would require increasing his current sales rate of one sale per fortnight to a total of two sales per fortnight. The additional sales commission and the bonuses that he would receive as a result of those extra sales would provide him with more than the additional money he needs.

2. He currently receives four qualified sales leads per fortnight from his employer. On average, the four leads result in three sales presentations and, on average, they result in one sale.
3. Until now, he has taken a very laid back attitude to his career as a sales person. He knows that he is in a position to create opportunity to make more sales by increasing his leads. He has decided that he will ask every person to whom he makes a sales presentation for referrals. He will also create additional opportunity by going through his employer's list of everyone who has bought a property from his company (whether sold by him or not) and make a service call on them to ensure they are satisfied with the property. By establishing rapport during the service call, he will create the added opportunity of asking them for referrals — the name and contact details of people they know and who they believe may be interested in buying a property and would benefit from doing so.
4. He knows his sales averages and that his sales have been created as a result of the leads received from his employer. He is confident that, in addition to the four leads per fortnight from his employer, he is capable of generating at least twelve referrals per fortnight from which he believes he will make at least one additional sale per fortnight and probably more.
5. He has decided that he will acquire the special knowledge he needs by gaining extra knowledge about the properties he is selling, including their potential for capital growth. He will also undertake sales training to become better at selling and closing sales.

He has decided that as a salesperson, he must become a lead generation machine and that he will develop and follow through on creating more leads. With additional referrals, he will create the potential to make additional sales. Without leads, he has nothing. Increased leads are his key to increased sales.

After taking into account all his considerations, the young man completes his Exercise 5 by formulating and writing his plan as follows:
1. I shall, in addition to the leads from my employer, obtain at least twelve referrals per fortnight from all my purchasers and prospective purchasers. I shall also make service calls on persons who have previously bought properties through me and through other salespersons engaged by my employer, establish rapport with them and obtain leads from them.
2. I will formulate new ideas through which to acquire more and more leads and will follow up on every one of them.
3. I shall make an average minimum of two sales every fortnight from the referrals I obtain and the leads provided to me by my employer.
4. I shall periodically undertake additional sales training to increase my sales ability.
5. I shall ensure that I gain a fully comprehensive knowledge from my employer of the properties I am selling including a full understanding of their potential for capital growth and their other financial advantages.
6. I shall save all the additional income I generate from my additional sales in a bank account, targeting a minimum savings of $20,000 per annum net after tax over the next five years until I have saved the $100,000 that I need. I will not spend any part of those savings until I have met my bank's criteria and qualified for a loan to assist me to purchase my home. I shall not use my savings for any purpose other than to enable me to purchase the property.
7. I shall, at the appropriate time, approach my bank and secure approval for a loan of $320,000 subject to valuation of the property I wish to purchase.
8. I shall regularly monitor the movement of sales prices in the residential property market. I know that by increasing my earnings, I will qualify to borrow a higher amount from the bank. If prices move up, so will valuations. If after taking these factors into

consideration, the cash shortfall that I must earn increases, I will first endeavour to increase my borrowings or, if necessary, extend my time period for achieving my goal.
9. *I will use what I have learnt from* Formula for Success in Life, Career and Business *to stay focused until I achieve my plan.*

The young man's dream has expanded. He is already thinking ahead and dreaming that when he has achieved his goal and bought his home, he'll not stop there. His next primary goal will be to buy an investment property and then another and another. He smiles as he thinks that in a few years when he drives down the road in his new Lamborghini, people will be saying: "Hey, there goes that rich dude who owns all those properties."

Example 2

An overweight middle-aged lady has been talking about losing weight for years and has finally decided to do something about it.

She has identified that if she tackles her weight problem herself, she has no material obstacles but only a mindset obstacle standing in her way — her lack of willpower. Her opportunity to acquire the right mindset is provided to her by *Formula for Success in Life, Career and Business*.

She must lose forty-eight kilograms in weight in the next twelve months. She has researched various diets and walking exercise regimes. She has written her entire diet menu for every day of the first twelve weeks to reduce her calorie intake. She has used her car to measure a distance of ten kilometres around the streets of her suburb starting at her front gate and back again. She has had a medical checkup and been encouraged by her doctor to follow her plan, taking it relatively easy at first and progressively increasing the distance and speed of her walks. Her doctor has also advised her to have regular medical checkups.

After taking into account all her considerations, she has completed her Exercise 5 by formulating and writing her plan as follows:

My plan starting tomorrow and for the next twelve weeks is:
1. *I shall stop buying and eating junk food.*
2. *I shall stop buying and drinking cans and bottles of soft drinks.*
3. *I shall eat three meals every day namely, breakfast, lunch and dinner, strictly in accordance with my diet menu ensuring that I limit the quantity of food I consume in accordance with the quantities I have noted in writing against each item in my menu and limit my daily calorie intake to not more than 1,200 calories per day.*
4. *Within my calorie limit, I shall allow myself a morning, afternoon and after dinner snack between meals of green tea and one diet biscuit.*
5. *I shall allow myself as much water and unsweetened green tea as I wish.*
6. *I shall exercise by walking every day to burn calories, gradually increasing my minimum daily walking distance until I reach my first target of ten kilometres per day and my speed to keep pace with my improving fitness.*
7. *I shall weigh myself every day before having my lunch and record my weight each day. I must and will achieve a weight loss of at least one kilogram per week on average for forty-eight weeks. My doctor has given me a medical check up and the OK to start my walking regime and I will continue to have regular medical checks to monitor my health.*
8. *I'll regularly read and follow Formula for* Success in Life, Career and Business *and drive myself to acquire a sufficient winner's mindset.*
9. *At the end of each twelve-week period I shall assess my weight loss results and have my doctor assess my fitness results and health.*

10. *At the end of each twelve-week period, I shall repeat what I have done during the previous twelve weeks and, subject to my doctor's advice, I may change my diet and increase the distance I walk each week.*

The woman smiles to herself and thinks that at the end of twelve months, she will be trim, taut, terrific and fit and maybe next year, she'll run her first marathon.

Example 3

A young girl, who has recently completed her secondary education, wishes to obtain a degree in veterinary science in order to follow her dream career as a veterinary surgeon.

She has identified her material obstacles as follows:
1. Not having a sufficiently high matriculation grade to gain admission to study for a veterinary science degree at Sydney University; and
2. Not having the cash to pay her University fees or support herself during her years as a student or to buy the textbooks she will need for her studies.

She has identified her opportunities as follows:
1. To gain admission to her desired degree by firstly gaining admission to initially study for a veterinary nursing degree at Sydney University. By doing this she will be entitled to gain admission to study for a degree in veterinary science by transferring to that course after she has passed a certain number of units towards her nursing degree. This will overcome the obstacle of an insufficient matriculation grade.
2. She has also identified that she is entitled to have her university fees paid by the government under its HECS-Help program; and

3. That her parents are happy for her to live at home, support her, pay for her textbooks and provide her with a weekly living allowance.

After taking into account all her considerations, she completes her Exercise 5 by formulating and writing her plan as follows:

My plan is clear:
1. *I shall use my matriculation grade to gain admission to study for a degree in veterinary nursing at Sydney University.*
2. *I shall study hard and as soon as I have passed a sufficient number of units towards my veterinary nursing degree I shall use them to gain admission by transferring to study for my veterinary science degree at Sydney University.*
3. *I shall apply for and be enrolled in the HECS-Help scheme in order to have the government pay my university fees.*
4. *I shall continue to live at home and accept my parents offer to support me while I'm at university and to buy my textbooks for me.*
5. *I shall prepare a study schedule at the start of every semester for each subject and study hard and, if ever I find myself not strictly adhering to my schedule, I shall use the information relating to gaining a sufficient winner's mindset as provided in* Formula for Success in Life, Career and Business *to get myself back on track.*

In looking forward to acquiring her degree, she dreams of working tirelessly to help animals. She smiles and whispers: "One day I shall be a Mother Teresa to all animals in need of medical help."

Example 4

A man in his thirties has decided to quit smoking.

He has identified that his obstacles are his lack of willpower and lack of a singularity of purposes to overcome his nicotine addiction. He has identified that his opportunities to overcome his obstacles to acquire a sufficient winner's mindset are provided in *Formula for Success in Life, Career and Business* and that once acquired, nothing is impossible.

After taking into account all his considerations, he completes his Exercise 5 by formulating and writing his plan as follows:

My plan is that starting tomorrow morning:
1. *I shall quit smoking, cold turkey.*
2. *I shall not drink alcohol until my craving for cigarettes has ceased because alcohol increases my craving and lowers my resolve.*
3. *I shall never smoke again.*
4. *If I feel my resolve is weakening, I'll read and re-read* Formula for Success in Life, Career and Business *on acquiring a sufficient winner's mindset and apply the information provided until I completely restore my resolve.*

He too smiles and says to himself: "And, when my breathing is back to normal, no one at my Club will beat me on the tennis court. No one. Once I've regained my title of 'Club Champion', I can go back to bragging about it at the Club's bar — just to annoy everyone."

Example 5

A husband and wife are business partners and operate a successful accountancy practice. They wish to double the current gross annual income of $1,500,000 earned by their practice, increasing it to $3,000,000 per annum.

They have identified that the obstacle they face is to earn an additional gross income of $1,5000,000 in fees every year. They must create the opportunity to overcome their obstacle by creating the means to increasing their client base until they earn an additional $1,500,000 every year in fees from their increased client base.

They discuss what needs to be done and decide that until they achieve their goal, the husband will devote himself to expanding their accountancy practice by recruiting a sufficient number of new clients from whom to earn the additional fees and, during that time, the wife will assume the role of practice manager and run the practice.

The average annual amount earned, by way of fees, from clients vary considerably and they determine that they will target clients at various fee ranges. The professional accountancy services they offer include, for the most part, auditing, taxation, business advice and general accounting.

They consider and make a written list of everything that must be done. They agree that they will discuss in detail what's necessary and jointly formulate their written plan.

After taking into account all their considerations and discussions, they complete their Exercise 5 by formulating and writing their plan as follows:

1. *Wife will immediately assume the role of practice manager of the firm and be responsible for running the practice.*
2. *Wife will engage an employment agency that specialises in recruiting professional staff to assist her to recruit and employ suitably qualified and experienced chartered accountants, one at a time, as required by the work increase.*
3. *Upon employing the first new accountant and in order to free husband to concentrate full time on expanding the practice, he will re-allocate the work that he currently undertakes to the accountants engaged by the firm.*
4. *Husband will contract an advertising and promotional expert to advise and assist him, to aggressively market and promote the accountancy practice (within the policy guidelines for chartered accountants). As part of the advertising and promotional campaign conducted on the internet and by other means, he will offer excellent*

incentives to companies and businesses to contact him and discuss the incentives and services offered.

5. In addition to the advertising and promotional campaign, husband will prepare a list of local companies and businesses that potentially fit the firm's client profile, research them to discover their respective CEOs and owners and research every new business that is opening or has recently opened in reasonably close proximity to the firm's office. He will also obtain referrals from clients to others who may require accountancy services.

6. Husband will prepare a letter introducing the practice, the services offered and excellent incentives inviting potential clients to use the accounting service. He will follow up on each letter with a telephone call to each person to whom a letter has been sent and endeavour to make an appointment to discuss the firm's offer and the benefits of engaging it to provide accountancy services required by the prospective client.

7. Husband will aggressively target and recruit new clients within the five following annual fee ranges:
Fee Range 1: Potential fee range of $100,000 plus.
Fee Range 2: Potential fee range of $50,000 plus.
Fee Range 3: Potential fee range of $20,000 plus.
Fee Range 4: Potential fee range of $10,000 plus.
Fee Range 5: Potential fee range of $5,000 plus or minus.

8. During the next three years, husband will recruit:
Within Fee Range 1: At lease 5 new clients.
Within Fee Range 2: At lease 10 new clients
Within Fee Range 3: At lease 10 new clients.
Within Fee Range 4: At lease 20 new clients.
Within Fee Range 5: At lease 20 new clients.

9. In order to ensure that husband will achieve his targets within the next three years, he must recruit at least:
One client in Fee Range 1 every 6 months.
Two clients in Fee Range 2 every 6 months.

Two clients in Fee Range 3 every 6 months.
Four clients in Fee Range 4 every 6 months.
Four clients in Fee Range 5 every 6 months.
10. Husband considers the targets he has set to be achievable, depending upon the success of his campaign, but he will adjust and improve his campaign, as necessary, depending upon his success rate, including regularly inviting CEOs and in-house accountants to lunch to discuss his firm's offer.
11. Husband will prepare and submit tenders for all accountancy work offered on tender, as he considers appropriate.
12. Husband and wife will rigorously devote themselves to respectively acquiring a sufficient winner's mindset through Formula for Success in Life, Career and Business *to ensure that they keep their plan on track at all times.*

They sit back after completing their plan and think: "When we have achieved the necessary target, we'll go back to running the practice for a couple of years and hone it to maximise profits. We will use our increased profits and potential for expansion to have the practice valued and then place it on the market for sale. It will all be a hugely worthwhile exercise, especially after selling the business and retiring to enjoy our dream of sailing around the Mediterranean on our yacht."

EXERCISE 5
To complete your written plan

This Exercise requires you to precisely formulate your plan.

You are asked to formulate and then precisely define in writing the plan that will enable you to fully and systematically achieve your goal. It should show how you will use your available material and mindset opportunities including those that you create and how you will gain and use the special material and mindset knowledge that you have or will acquire in order to use those opportunities to overcome your material and mindset obstacles and attain your primary goal.

Please read and understand the information provided in this chapter including the five examples as many times as you may need. When satisfied that you have an understanding of the information you need and what is expected of you, please complete Exercise 5.

After you have formulated and properly defined your plan you will know what you must do, step-by-step, in order to attain your primary goal. As stated earlier, you may discover that there are various interim goals and targets to be achieved along the way. If so, incorporate them as part of your plan as you become aware of them and achieve them step by step.

Your guidelines for completing this Exercise and, in doing so, completing your plan are:

1. Firstly, think carefully and consider every item that you consider should be included in your plan to enable you to achieve your primary goal.
2. In thinking about them, understand that you have already identified your obstacles and the opportunities that you must possess in order to overcome them. You have also identified what, if any, special knowledge you must or should acquire.
3. Your plan involves the highly important step of setting down what you must do on a step-by-step basis in order to acquire and to use the opportunities you have identified in order to overcome your obstacles and attain your primary goal. It should include what must be done to acquire the special knowledge you need.
4. Your plan is a simple, but very necessary course of action that you must follow in order to achieve your primary goal.

On completion of Exercise 5, you will have formulated and precisely defined your plan in writing, including its material and mindset aspects.

When satisfied with the final written draft of your plan, it is your answer to Exercise 5.

Please write or type your answer on a blank sheet of A4 paper headed "My Plan".

There is of course nothing to prevent you from expanding your plan with further items in the future, if you discover other items that need to be included.

In conclusion

At the end of completing Exercise 5, you will have completed another vital step in the process of achieving your primary goal. You will have completed the written plan that you must follow, never quitting until you attain your primary goal.

Always remember, as stated earlier, it is relatively easy to prepare a plan, it's much more difficult to follow that plan every day, week, month and year, never quitting until you achieve your goal. As part of your journey you must acquire a sufficient winner's mindset, because it will never permit you to quit until you achieve that goal.

Your answers to this Exercise 5 are the fifth part of your 'blueprint' for achieving success.

It is now a question of doing what's necessary to acquire a sufficient winner's mindset. With your plan and the necessary winner's mindset, nothing will stop you except matters outside your control.

File the completed pages in your folder entitled: "Achieving My Primary Goal".

As you complete each Exercise your folder has grown and it now also contains your completed written plan of how you will achieve your primary goal, interim goals and targets.

DIVISION 2
THE WINNER'S MINDSET

6
A SUFFICIENT WINNER'S MINDSET

Fundamental Principle Six
Understand what is a sufficient winner's mindset and what it can do for you. Without it, you will not have the singularity of purpose you need to pursue a goal, especially a goal that may only be achieved over a long time period. With it, you will be driven to doggedly pursue your goal, never quitting until you achieve it.

A sufficient winner's mindset is a state of mind that gives you the singularity of purpose to unwaveringly follow your plan every step of the way, day by day, week by week, month by month, year by year, come what may, never quitting until you successfully achieve your primary goal and every other interim goal and target along the way.

It is an essential element of *Formula for Success in Life, Career and Business*.

This chapter explains and provides you with a preliminary understanding of the various elements that constitute a winner's mindset. The various chapters that follow will assist you to identify the strengths, attributes and traits you possess and the degree to which you possess them. They will also assist you to acquire the strengths, attributes and traits that you do not posses and to strengthen those that require strengthening.

It's relatively easy to develop and write your plan. It's much more difficult to consistently follow and work it, never quitting until you bring it to a successful conclusion. Those who have the necessary singularity of purpose will do so. Those without it will usually quit before achieving success.

When you acquire a sufficient winner's mindset, you will acquire the necessary singularity of purpose that enables you to achieve your primary goal. If you don't already possess that singular mindset, you must acquire it. If you possess it to a limited degree, you must strengthen it. The information in this book will show you how.

A written plan is an essential tool that is a first step towards the successful achievement of your primary goal and all interim goals and targets. But remember that your plan is merely a means through which to achieve whatever you seek to accomplish. It keeps you on track. It is the roadmap outlining the path you must follow. If you walk the path, it will lead you to successfully achieve your goal. It's entirely up to you.

You must not only talk the talk, you must also walk the walk. In other words, you must take the necessary action and work every step of your plan until you reach your goal. It's not the plan itself that get's you to your destination, but the relentless never quit execution of your plan that gets you there. It is your mindset and not the plan that drives you.

Never believe the so-called gurus who will have you believe that if you hope fervently enough, some cosmic or other force will miraculously convert your dream into reality. They are delusional and so are their gullible followers. It's a convenient excuse for not getting off their backsides and doing the work that's necessary to achieve success. It's much easier to lay back and do nothing in the belief that if you wish for it strongly enough, money will be attracted to you and start pouring into your bank account. Yes, some so-called gurus really teach this nonsense and many people believe it. Unless you are one of the lucky few who inherit a fortune or win the lottery, there is usually no easy road to riches or success. You must take whatever action is necessary to get there.

Success is achieved through hard work. Yes, wishing fervently for what you want to achieve may help focus your mind, but nothing will eventuate from a fervent wish, no matter how much you focus on it, unless you put in the hard work to achieve it. There is no substitute for formulating a written plan and working it tirelessly until you succeed. If you do that, you will achieve success and if you include a saving plan, your bank account will grow. Simply wishing and visualising, regardless of how fervently, will achieve nothing other than help you focus.

Can you imagine an athlete, who wants to win a gold medal at the next Olympic Games, sitting at home and every day fervently wishing and hoping to win gold instead of getting out there and doing the necessary training? It just does not happen! Wishing and dreaming without the necessary action achieves very little, if anything. Fervent wishing coupled with persistent hard work is the winning formula. Fervent wishing helps engender the impetus and drive you need to keep you focused, but it's persistent hard work that produces the necessary result.

The problem is that many of us do not have the capacity to follow our plan through to a successful conclusion. Life interferes, we get distracted, change our minds and either quit or keep procrastinating, never quite getting around to doing what must be done, always putting off until tomorrow what must be done today. Of course, tomorrow seldom, if ever, comes.

Adhering to and relentlessly working your plan takes a high level of commitment. Very few people have the singularity of purpose that brings that level of commitment. This is why it's essential, for most of us, to acquire it. By acquiring a sufficient winner's mindset, you acquire the singularity of purpose necessary to pursue and ensure a successful conclusion to your every endeavour.

If you write a plan, acquire whatever special knowledge you may need and add a sufficient winner's mindset, nothing except circumstances beyond your control, such as ill-health, will hold you back from achieving success in life, career, business or whatever other endeavour you pursue.

A sufficient winner's mindset gives you the power to translate your plan into reality. It enables you to action and work your plan, never quitting until you achieve success.

As the first preliminary step to understanding the winner's mindset, let's first take a brief look at the various character strengths, attributes and traits that are either essential to or will greatly assist you to acquire and maintain the winner's mindset. They include:
- Eight essential strengths;
- Eight driving strengths;
- Eight supportive strengths;
- Five leadership attributes;
- Four pleasing personality traits; and
- Good health.

Once you have a better knowledge and understanding of the various strengths, attributes and traits that constitute the winner's mindset, you will be in a much better position to positively assess which of them you possess and the extent or degree to which you possess them. In turn those assessments will enable you to ascertain which of them you do not possess and, if you do, whether you possess them at an unacceptably low level.

Nobody knows you better than you know yourself. You are therefore the best person to make those assessments. However, in making them, you must be scrupulously honest with yourself.

You cannot lie to yourself. There is no room here for self-deception or self-delusion. Unfortunately some of us possess a tendency to be self-delusional and for that reason do not readily admit our faults when undertaking a self-assessment.

For that reason, it's useful to have another person do an independent assessment of your strengths, attributes and traits and to use that assessment as a reality check of your self assessment.

The person best suited to assist you with the reality check is usually a close family member or friend. Apart from yourself, they should know you best. Their assessment will counter balance any tendency in you towards self-deception or self-delusion, providing they are honest and don't simply tell you what they think you wish to hear and provided you accept what they say in a rational balanced manner.

Question and answer forms to conduct the various self-analyses and reality checks are contained in Division 3.

The eight essential strengths

The eight essential strengths are:
- Desire;
- Determination;
- Passion;
- Positivity;
- Focus;
- Persistence;
- Commitment; and
- Decisiveness.

Those strengths are the powerhouse of your mind. Collectively they are the essential elements of a winner's mindset that will drive you to successfully achieve your primary goal.

The first four, namely, desire, determination, passion and positivity are the essential forces that compel you to go after what you want, come what may. The second four namely focus, persistence, commitment and decisiveness are those elements that bolster the first four, giving you the impetus, the support and the single mindedness that prevents you from deviating from the achievement of your goal.

Your desire must be a fervent desire. Without that fervent desire, you will not be driven to the extent needed to achieve what you want. A mere wish or whim is insufficient. It must be an intense, deep desire.

When you have that intensity of desire, it translates into determination, especially if you encourage it. The greater your desire for your goal, the greater will be your determination to achieve it. A fervent desire will result in a fierce determination that is as intense as your desire. The two strengths feed off and fuel each other and when they unite in your mind they have the capacity to become a formidable force.

Intensity of desire is really another way of describing passion. It must be so intense as to be an unbridled passion. In turn, that degree of passion engenders positivity and drive.

Together, those four elements are a powerful formidable force. Fervent desire, fierce determination, unbridled passion and powerful positivity are the four essential character strengths that make you unstoppable.

If you think that the case for the first four essential strengths has been overstated, then think again. What you need in order to overcome your mindset obstacles is a sufficient winner's mindset. You cannot overstate the intensity or degree to which you must strive to acquire them. You must use your best endeavours and all your powers to do everything that is reasonably necessary to attain and maintain those four strengths at the highest possible level.

Achieve and maintain them at a high level and nothing will stop you. Once you have them, maintain them and work on strengthening them. They will be your most powerful mindset strengths.

The next four essential strengths, namely, unrelenting focus, unswerving persistence, unwavering commitment and unshakeable decisiveness will hugely assist by bolstering your efforts to achieve those first four essential strengths.

When you have that unrelenting focus and unswerving persistence, never quitting, driving you to consistently follow your plan until your goal is achieved, you will have taken a giant step forward. In turn, they lead you to an unwavering commitment to achieve your goal. Add unshakeable decisiveness to the mix and you will hugely bolster your chances of success.

Achieve and maintain the eight essential strengths at a sufficiently intense level and nothing, other than factors beyond your control, will ever stop you!

The eight driving strengths

The eight driving strengths are:
- Drive;
- Proactivity;
- Motivation;
- Ambition;
- Willpower;
- Creativity;
- Intuition; and
- Curiosity.

These are the strengths that constitute your driving force, compelling you to build intensity and use your essential strengths until you successfully achieve your primary goal.

All eight driving strengths are highly effective in driving you to achieve and maintain your essential strengths. The first five, namely, drive, proactivity, motivation, ambition and willpower will keep you on track and underpin your desire to achieve. The next three namely, creativity, intuition and curiosity are elements that ignite and fuel the power of positive proactivity.

Always be particularly aware of the driving strengths and remember that if you do not possess them or any of them, that lack may prove to be counter-productive. For example, if you do not possess willpower but instead are weak willed, lacking the drive and always procrastinating or taking the easy way out, how will you ever succeed? Lack of willpower sows the seeds of failure.

Each of the driving strengths and all other character strengths and positive attributes play an important role and their importance should never be underestimated.

The eight supportive strengths

The eight supportive strengths are:
- Integrity;
- Reliability;
- Balance;
- Confidence;
- Optimism;
- Enthusiasm;
- Self reliance; and
- Adaptability.

These are the strengths that constitute a strong supportive base. They are the foundation on which your mind is able to build and intensify your essential and driving strengths.

Regardless of our goals, whether in life, career, business or any other pursuit, you seldom, if ever, live in isolation. In one way or the other, you rely on others for their support and others rely on you for yours.

The business world, in particular, is reliant on the goodwill of others including clients, customers, suppliers, bankers and financiers. The first three supportive strengths, namely, integrity, reliability and balance are essential in building trust in others. If you show that you are honest, a person who keeps his or her word and, if you have a balanced personality, not prone to erratic behaviour, others will increasingly trust you. You will build their trust in you. They are the foundational slabs for building a solid supportive business base. In a similar manner, you will come to trust others for the same reason.

The next five supportive strengths, namely, confidence, optimism, enthusiasm, self-reliance and adaptability, not only have a positive effect on how others will react to you, but are also important inner strengths. The first four will keep you buoyant and build your positivity whilst the fifth, namely adaptability, will serve to always keep you one step ahead of the game.

The five leadership attributes

The five leadership attributes are:
- Leadership qualities;
- Good communication skills;
- Organisational skills;
- Hard work; and
- Intelligence.

They are positive character attributes that will greatly assist you in your every endeavour, whether in business or otherwise. They will assist you to achieve your primary goal and every other interim goal and target that you set yourself.

In order to achieve any goal or target, you must take control. You must lead the way. You must be the master or mistress of your own destiny. You cannot expect others to do it for you. You can however gain the support and assistance of others and you will achieve this much more effectively if you exhibit leadership qualities.

You must be or become a strong effective leader and your leadership qualities will be greatly enhanced if you are a good communicator and also possess strong organisational skills.

When you add hard work and intelligence to your other leadership qualities, the mix is substantially strengthened.

Little is achieved without hard work. It not only gets things done, but by being a hard worker you lead by example. Of course, far more is achieved if you work intelligently in order to achieve the best results. Firstly think and secondly relentlessly take whatever action is necessary.

The four positive personality traits

The four positive personality traits are:
- A pleasant personality;
- Tact;
- Tolerance; and
- A good sense of humour.

A pleasant personality will assist you not only with enhancing your leadership qualities but also in building good relations with others. Others much prefer to deal with a person who has a pleasant personality rather than with someone who is unpleasant, overbearing, self-opinionated or a bully.

As part of your personality traits, you should also have tact, tolerance and a good sense of humour. They will prove to be a distinct advantage.

Good health

Good physical and mental health is essential. As distinct from strengths, attributes and traits, your health attributes include good physical and mental health and your general well being.

Regardless of how intense your other strengths, attributes and traits may be, there are many goals that simply cannot be achieved without good health. For example, if you are debilitated by physical ill health, perhaps even bedridden, there is much that you can never achieve regardless of how strong your mindset may be. Imagine being bedridden with emphysema. In that case, you cannot walk to the top of Mount Everest, no matter how much you desire to do so. Exercise your imagination and you will no doubt think of many other examples where ill health would undoubtedly prevent you from attaining specific physical and mindset goals.

If you possess a sufficient winner's mindset and good physical and mental health, nothing will stop you. You will possess what it takes to not only achieve your primary goal but every other goal and target that you set yourself from time to time whether in life, career, business or whatever other pursuit you choose.

The power of your mind

Let's return for a moment to the person striving to be an elite athlete, an Olympic gold medallist or other sporting world champion. Athletes get to the top of their field by formulating a plan. In their case it usually includes a training program. They are driven by the desire to be the best in the world in their particular sporting field. Those who develop a sufficient winner's mindset and are driven by the determination to relentlessly stick to their training programs are the ones who have the best chance of success.

You will succeed if you adopt the same proven formula of a world champion athlete.

The difference is that in your case, you are probably not competing against others to become the world's best in your field. Unless you too are an elite world-class athlete, you are probably simply striving to be successful in your particular field. Your goal will probably be more modest than that of someone striving to be a world champion. Instead of competing against others, you will more likely be competing against yourself to overcome any weaknesses that are holding you back from attaining your primary goal. Regardless of your primary goal, the formula for achieving it is the same. Form a plan, learn to never quit and keep going until you succeed.

Assuming you have already completed your written plan, your next step will be to take whatever action is necessary to carry out each step of your plan and to relentlessly work it until you successfully achieve your goal.

The question to ask yourself at this stage is: Do I have a sufficient winner's mindset to unfailing do everything in my plan, step-by-step, until I successfully achieve my goal?

At this early stage, you will only be able to answer that question from your gut. Do you honestly feel and believe that you have the singularity of purpose to unwavering pursue your goal until you achieve it? Do you honestly feel and believe that if you find yourself deviating from your purpose, you are prepared to do whatever is necessary to acquire a sufficient winner's mindset, to keep yourself on track? If your gut tells you that you are, answer the questions with a "yes". Based on your gut feeling, you are ready to proceed.

Later in this book, when you answer the self-analysis questions in Chapter 13 and have a family member or friend answer the reality check questions in Chapter 14, please revisit your preliminary answers to the questions in the immediately preceding two paragraphs and check the accuracy of your initial gut reaction.

The difference between winners and losers is that winners work their plan until they achieve what they want. Loser's do not. Instead, they allow themselves to be diverted or they quit. The difference is their state of mind. Winners have a sufficient winner's mindset. Losers do not. By acquiring and maintaining the necessary mindset you transform yourself into a winner for the rest of your life.

It's all in your mind. You have the power to control your mind and your thoughts. Never underestimate the power of your mind. Never underestimate the importance of ensuring that you always retain the power of control over your mind and the ability to organise your thoughts.

Your character is defined by the thoughts that are predominantly in your mind. You and your mind are inseparable. Your mindset and your good health are highly important factors in achieving success.

In order to guarantee yourself a life of success and abundance you must acquire and maintain a sufficient winner's mindset. This book provides you with everything you need in order to do that. With the singularity of purpose that a sufficient winner's mindset will give you, you will have the power to follow through and successfully achieve every goal, every target and every plan that you set for yourself now and in the future.

Attain and maintain a sufficient winner's mindset and you will guarantee yourself success and abundance!

Napoleon Hill once very correctly told us that whatever your mind can conceive and you can believe, you can achieve. Conceive, believe and achieve.

Your only limitations are those that you impose upon yourself in your mind by your thoughts. You must have or must develop the power to control your mind and develop positive thoughts that stop you doubting your ability and placing limitations upon yourself. Develop that power and use it. It will be the most important asset of your life. It will empower you beyond your expectations. However, you should always endeavour to keep your expectations realistic.

Success won't come to you. You must make it happen. And sometimes, to make it happen, you must acquire the special knowledge that you need

For example, suppose your dream is to dive off a tall cliff and fly, to soar across the landscape and land safely in a distant paddock.

If you share your dream with your friends and family, apart from most of them thinking that you've gone completely bonkers, their immediate reaction, whilst sadly shaking their heads in disbelief, is probably going to be, "Sorry, but that's Impossible".

But, you and I know that nothing is impossible. Man's horizons expand with each successive generation at an ever-increasing rate. A few years ago, wing suits were not invented. Today, people use them to dive off cliffs and fly.

There are at least two ways you could pursue your dream.

One way would be to dress up as Superman or Wonder Woman, climb to the top of a tall cliff and dive off. Unfortunately you are not going to fly. Instead, you'll make a horrible mess of yourself and your family and friends will probably end up having to scrape what's left of you, off the rocks below.

Alternatively, you could take a more sensible approach. You could buy a wing suit, learn the theory of flying in one and undertake the necessary training until you are proficient. Now that you've gained the special knowledge you need, if you then climb the cliff, don your wing suit and dive off, you'll fly, soaring across the landscape.

But diving off a cliff in a wing suit is not something everyone can or wants to do. Only those who are totally committed, absolutely determined and have the courage to dive off the cliff will achieve their goal.

You not only need the special knowledge to successfully fly in a wing suit, but the mindset necessary to dive off the cliff. When you combine the two, namely, the special knowledge and a sufficient winner's mindset, you have the formula that will drive you to take the action and achieve your goal of flying, of diving off the cliff and soaring over the landscape to land safely in your chosen paddock.

It's exactly the same with achieving your primary goal and every future primary goal that you have. At the end of the day, what brings you success is having a sufficient winner's mindset, ensuring you have whatever special knowledge you may need and, of course, having good health.

When you have completed writing your plan, you will be standing on the brink of launching yourself into action and step-by-step working your plan unwaveringly and tenaciously until you attain your goal. Each step in your plan is an interim goal or target and achieving a sufficient winner's mindset is one of them.

You are now ready to acquire a sufficient winner's mindset. Study and implement the relevant information contained in this book until you do.

With the singularity of purpose afforded to you by a sufficient winner's mindset, once acquired, you will not hesitate to follow your plan. Your mind will not permit you to hesitate. Procrastination will have been banished from your life. You will be driven forward, compelled to take action, compelled to drive yourself to achieve every step of your plan within your allocated time period.

In essence, your winner's mindset will be an unwavering obsession to achieve your primary goal and every other interim goal and target along the way. It is essential.

Never quit

Finally a few words on the absolute importance of never quitting until you achieve your goal.

If you never quit in your mind, you can never be beaten. You are never beaten until your mind accepts defeat. You may be physically overcome, but you are never beaten until you mentally quit.

Nothing is impossible. Persistence and unwavering determination are two of the fundamental keys to achieving success. Winners never quit. Only losers do. If at first you don't succeed, try, try and try again and success will come to you.

Stay positive and regardless of how many setbacks you suffer, Never Quit!

In conclusion

Your effort, your time, your dogged unwavering application of the underlying principles of the formula contained in this book is what you need to succeed.

Acquiring and maintaining a sufficient winner's mindset, hard work, gaining the special knowledge you need and having good physical and mental health will get you there.

Never believe the nonsense written about success materialising or money coming to you if you envision it strongly enough. It never happens. Only those who are delusional or are looking for a lazy or easy way out could ever believe such nonsense.

Thinking hard about what you want will help you focus on achieving your goal, but focus will not of itself bring you success.

A sufficient winner's mindset will drive you, buoyed by your unwavering determination, to do what you must do to achieve what you want. It's what you do and how you do it that will bring you success.

Nothing is impossible if you have the special knowledge you need, good health and a sufficient winner's mindset that will drive you to keep going step after step with absolute persistence and dogged determination until you achieve your required goal. You must keep going and never quit regardless of how many temporary setbacks you may experience on the way.

It is the action you take and the hard work you put in that will bring you success. One of the fundamental principles of *Formula for Success in Life, Career and Business* is that you never quit until you succeed. Believe me. I know this to be absolutely true.

I've proven it to myself. By never quitting, you will prove it to yourself.

You have nothing to lose and everything to gain. Simply read, understand, inwardly digest and apply what you learn in this book.

Get stuck into it! Just do it.

7
YOUR ESSENTIAL STRENGTHS

Fundamental Principle Seven
Understand the essential strengths you must possess, acquire or strengthen in order to acquire a sufficient winner's mindset.

You have learnt that a sufficient winner's mindset is a state of mind that gives you the singularity of purpose to unwaveringly follow your plan every step of the way, never quitting until you achieve your primary goal.

You have also learnt that there are eight essential strengths that help constitute the winner's mindset:
- Desire;
- Determination;
- Passion;
- Positivity;
- Focus;
- Persistence;
- Commitment; and
- Decisiveness.

Of the essential strengths, the first four, namely, desire, determination, passion and positivity, are absolutely essential and the next four, namely, focus, persistence, commitment and decisiveness are of the utmost importance.

If you do not already possess the essential strengths or any one or more of them, they are each capable of being acquired. If you already possess one or more of them, you may strengthen them.

As part of the process of acquiring a sufficient winner's mindset, you should firstly undertake the self-analysis process to identify which of the essential strengths you possess and the degree to which you possess them. Once completed you should then undertake the reality check process to verify the accuracy or otherwise of your self-analysis. You will find the process for undertaking the self-analysis set out in Chapter 13 and the process for the reality check in Chapter 14.

On completion of the two (2) processes, you should be in a position to decide which essential strengths that you possess and the degree to which you possess them. You will of course also determine which essential strengths you do not possess and need to acquire or strengthen.

The answers gained after undertaking the processes are necessary in guiding you to acquire the essential strengths.

Before undertaking the processes, let's firstly obtain an understanding of the essential strengths in the context of a sufficient winner's mindset.

The essential strengths

The following is a brief explanation of each of the essential strengths:

1. Desire

In order to achieve success, you must desire it to such an extent that your every other wish or desire fades away.

It must be a fervent desire, an all-consuming desire to achieve your primary goal and not just another wish, whim or passing fancy. It must be an intense desire bordering on obsession. You must so fervently desire to successfully achieve your primary goal that, for you, there is no alternative — no other option. Your desire must be so great that, if necessary, you are prepared to burn all bridges behind you, leaving yourself nowhere else to go. It is a desire that sits at your very core. You are emotionally attached to it. The desire to attain your primary goal becomes the very reason for your existence.

It is your most important desire. It is the force that will drive you to attain your primary goal, come what may.

Unless you have that desire, none of the other essential strengths come into play. You won't pursue your goal unless you have a really compelling desire to attain it.

It's not just another wish, whim, passing fancy or something that you don't really care whether you attain or not, or something that you'll make little, if any effort, to pursue.

Desire is one of the most powerful essential strengths in the winner's mindset.

2. Determination

It must be a fierce determination to achieve your primary goal that is so strong and focused that you permit nothing else to interfere with it. Fervent desire breeds fierce determination.

They feed off and fuel each other. Each strengthens the other. They unite to become a formidable unstoppable force and when you possess them, nothing, except circumstances beyond your control, will divert you from the singularity of purpose that drives you to achieve your primary goal.

It's a determination that is so strong that it drives you to single-mindedly and persistently keep going in pursuit of your primary goal, never to be diverted until you achieve it.

Fierce determination and fervent desire are two of your most important essential strengths. If you have them, they come together and drive you to attain your primary goal, come what may.

3. Passion

In the context of the winner's mindset, passion refers to an intense unbridled emotion engendered by your fervent desire and fierce determination — a passion that drives you to pursue your primary goal until it is successfully achieved.

It will give you the commitment you need to unswervingly follow your plan with dedicated conviction. If you are passionate about what you are doing, it often means that you love what you are doing. To love what you are doing is one of your most compelling motivators, because you are not just driven by your mind but also by your heart.

Passion will prevent you from compromising and settling for second best. When you are passionate about achieving your goal, your passion will heighten your positivity and determination to achieve it. The greater your passion, the greater will be your drive to follow and action every step of your plan until you achieve your goal.

Passion can also be highly contagious.

You will find, when supporting a worthwhile cause (and depending upon your commitment to that cause), your passion often tends to be much more intense. The drive generated by such intense passion incentivises others to follow and support your cause and the support of others makes it easier to achieve your goal.

Suppose your primary goal is to have legislation introduced in your country to abolish the use of palm oil in all food, personal care and other products because palm oil growers are destroying natural habitat and driving orangutans and many other species of wildlife to extinction. Your passion for the cause enhances the intensity with which you deliver your message. The passion with which you pursue your goal intensifies your drive to follow your plan. As a result, others are incentivised by your passion and are driven to follow and help your cause. Your task to achieve your goal becomes easier with the help of others.

Passion is an essential strength that you must have if you are to acquire a sufficient winner's mindset. Passion, positivity and determination are closely related and work in close harmony, serving to intensify proactive drive, forcing you to follow and action every step of your plan until you achieve your goal.

4. Positivity

It must be powerful positivity and belief that all things will turn out in your favour.

Powerful positivity is an attitude. It is a never say die state of mind, because you are absolutely certain that you will succeed. An intensely positive mindset does not accept defeat. Regardless of how many times you may be physically beaten, your intensely positive mindset will not permit your mind to accept defeat and throw in the towel. It makes you keep fighting, time and time again, never quitting until you succeed. It is an attitude that will never permit you to accept defeat. Every time you are knocked down, it will make you stand up and fight. It will not permit you to quit. It will drive you and never permit you to cease until you successfully achieve whatever goal you have set yourself to achieve.

The circumstances of any situation may cause you to react positively or negatively. It's your choice. If you react negatively, it is because you choose to do so. You may just as easily choose to react positively. Indeed, you must choose to act positively and avoid negativity at all costs. You must achieve such a positive attitude that you will never choose to act negatively.

There is the old question. Is a glass half full or half empty? How do you view it? It's a question that helps determine whether you think positively or negatively. Which view do you take? The positive half full view or the negative view that the glass is half empty?

A positive decisive mind will enable you to turn every temporary setback that you encounter (and you are likely to encounter many) into an advantage. Do this by analysing your every mistake that contributed to every temporary setback you encountered. Learn from them and never make the same mistake twice. Use this methodology always remembering that failure does not exist in your world. They are not failures but only temporary setbacks that you turn to your advantage by learning from them.

A positive decisive mind is a requisite for anyone seeking to acquire or strengthen his or her essential strengths or to attain any goal.

5. Focus

Focus is the power to concentrate your entire attention on one particular matter at a time to the exclusion of all other irrelevant or interfering thoughts.

In the context of the winner's mindset it is the power and ability to focus for long periods of time on what must be done to achieve your primary goal to the exclusion of all other conflicting thoughts and goals. It is an intense ability to concentrate, allowing nothing to divert you from your single-minded purpose.

The ability to acquire that degree of focus may be learned and achieved by anyone with the desire and determination to acquire it. When acquired, it will be a positive strength that will greatly enhance your ability to attain your primary goal and all subsequent goals. If you acquire the power to completely focus on relevant constructive thoughts while shutting out all interfering thoughts that may sidetrack you, are well on the way to achieving anything and everything you set your mind to achieve.

A person without the power of focus seldom, if ever, achieves his or her goal and this is especially true when a goal is only achievable over time and, as a result, the required focus must be consistently exercised over a prolonged period of time.

6. Persistence

It must be unswerving persistence, an unwavering steadfastness or singularity of purpose to persistently and tenaciously pursue your plan until you achieve your primary goal. It causes you to stay with and consistently follow and work through every aspect of your plan, concentrating your mind on one aspect of the plan at a time, to the exclusion of all other distractions. It is a stubborn resolve that drives you to unfailingly take whatever action is necessary day after day to persistently and consistently follow your plan, completing every task that must be undertaken, never allowing yourself to be sidetracked.

It is especially necessary when striving to achieve every task-oriented goal.

Consistent perseverance is an important strength and a key factor in accomplishing your goal. It is a discipline that may be learned and harnessed to ensure success in anything and everything you choose to accomplish.

Never underestimate the power of persistence. Get yourself into the groove and stay there until you succeed. Don't deviate or allow yourself to be deviated by others or by your own thoughts.

During good times and bad, persistence enables you to consistently work through your plan, dotting every "i" and crossing every "t", relentlessly focusing on and persistently pursuing your goal day-by-day, week-by-week, month-by-month and year-by-year, never quitting until you achieve it.

7. Commitment

You must be totally committed to achieving your primary goal.

You don't get what you want by simply wishing for it. You can only be sure of success if you are one hundred percent dedicated to achieving what you want. Unless you are fully committed to follow your plan, you considerably lessen your chances of turning your desire into reality.

Many people never fully commit to anything meaningful or worthwhile. What they see as commitment may be nothing more than a mere interest in or wish for some passing fancy — a mere transitory commitment, here today and gone tomorrow. It is simply not enough. Nothing short of total commitment will suffice.

Commitment goes beyond a mere interest in or a wish for something. To totally commit to achieving your desired outcome, you must block out all other possible alternatives and focus all your attention and efforts on the one definite outcome that you fervently desire. You must doggedly focus on achieving you intended outcome every day, week, month and year, as proves necessary, until you achieve it.

Only through total commitment will you achieve your desired outcome. In turn, each step that you successfully achieve towards the attainment of your particular goal or target encourages you and in so doing, strengthens your commitment.

When you commit you must be prepared to burn all bridges behind you and leave yourself with no alternative other than to pursue one clear path towards your desired outcome, never quitting until you achieve it. It takes that extreme singularity of purpose. You allow yourself no other alternative. It is a hard decision to make and even harder to execute.

However, when you do get to that position, there is no alternative. Either you have what it takes or you don't. There are no second measures. Your commitment must be absolutely unwavering. You must be proactive and never back down no matter what problems arise and you must do everything necessary to achieve your goal.

When you commit to achieving your desire, you must have the highest level of determination and passion. Only then will you overcome every doubt you encounter during difficult moments along the way.

You must fully commit to making a decision and abide by it, come what may. You must have whole-hearted commitment. You must have the necessary singularity of purpose. With it will come an improved ability to seek out and identify opportunities and the impetus to take more risks along your pathway to success. You achieve this thought process because in your mind there are now no other possibilities or alternate paths. You have left yourself with only two options — success or failure. For anyone with the necessary winner's mindset, failure is never an option.

Failure is too painful to contemplate. And so, you must persist and drive yourself, seizing every opportunity that presents itself, taking whatever risks are necessary, until you attain your goal.

It's not always about achieving your goal quickly. It may take months or even years to achieve your primary goal. You may need to frequently make many small commitments along the way to achieving your ultimate goal. You may find it necessary to develop new habits or skills and to firstly complete smaller enabling tasks on the way.

Every time you make a commitment to yourself, you are making a promise to yourself that you'll do something towards reaching your goal. You must follow through on every commitment you make — however large or small. You must never fail to successfully complete each commitment. And, if at first you fail in your attempts, you must try, try and try again until you succeed. That is your commitment. In doing so, you are conditioning your brain to never accept failure and to never quit until you attain your goal.

8. Decisiveness

It must be unrelenting decisiveness.

A keen unrelenting decisive mind is an essential ingredient of the mindset that you need to develop. It is a quality that helps you to quickly assess every situation or problem that arises and to positively and decisively find a solution. Under all circumstances, it causes you to act without undue delay to decisively and to expediently resolve every situation or problem as it arises.

It is an unrelenting quality that will not permit you to quit but rather will drive you to seek out and find the answer with which to decisively overcome every situation or problem you encounter.

Not every decision you will be required to make will be easy. Not every decision made under pressure will necessarily be the correct or best decision. No one is infallible. Where an erroneous decision is made or where a decision is not necessarily the best one, a decisive mind will enable you to quickly asses the error or shortfall and make whatever decision is necessary to rectify it. A decisive mind must possess the power of adaptability. A quick positive, decisive and adaptable mind is best, but decisions must only be made after proper and due consideration has been given and must never be rash.

A person with a decisive mind will also abide by his or her decisions and is not prone to being fickle or to constantly change course or be over-reactive. A decisive mind assists in creating persistence. A person with a decisive mind remains cool, calm and collected under pressure. A person with a decisive mind will usually seize control when a crisis arises. It is a mark of strong leadership.

If you are seen by others to have a decisive mind, you will gain leadership credibility in their eyes.

In summary

A fervent desire to achieve your primary goal is the key. A mere wish or whim will not hack it. When your fervent desire is fired by a fierce determination to achieve you goal and is underpinned by intense passion and powerful positivity, your mind will never permit you to quit. Achieve them and you would have already forged and welded together the four most essential and most important strengths of a sufficient winner's mindset.

When you achieve that and add focus, persistence, commitment and decisiveness to the mix, you will have laid the foundation for and provided the impetus that will make you an unstoppable force. You will indeed be a winner.

Reflect for a moment. It's a big ask — a big task. It's hard work. Long hours. However, it's what every Olympic or other world champion must do. They must have the desire and determination and the other essential strengths if they wish to be the world champion in their chosen sporting field. They must have the singularity of purpose and never quit until they WIN! They must be prepared to do whatever is necessary, within the right context, until they taste success. They must set themselves a plan or training program and relentlessly follow it until one day they stand tall on the podium, a gold medal dangling from a ribbon around their necks — winners and world champions.

Formula for Success in Life, Career and Business follows the same path and applies the same criteria to ensure you succeed and that you are a winner in life, career, business, wealth creation or whatever other pursuit you choose. It is a formula proven over and over again by the world's elite athletes. You must have or develop the desire, determination and the other essential strengths, formulate a plan and persistently follow it, absolutely believing that you will win.

In addition to competing against others, elite athletes must also compete against the demons within, such as lethargy, indecisiveness, procrastination and many more. Like an elite athlete, you want to be a winner. Like an elite athlete, you must also battle and overcome your shortcomings and inner demons to ensure you attain success.

By following *Formula for Success in Life, Career and Business*, you will guarantee yourself success and you will emerge a winner in whatever you undertake.

If there is one common essential thread to the necessary winner's mindset, it is singularity of purpose.

In conclusion

Please ensure that you understand all the essential strengths that you must acquire and how having them will help you.

By undertaking the self analysis process and the reality check process provided to you in Chapters 13 and 14, you will identify those essential strengths that you have, those that you do not and those that you possess to a limited level and that need strengthening.

8
YOUR DRIVING STRENGTHS

Fundamental Principle Eight
Understand the driving strengths that will assist you to gain the essential strengths and a sufficient winner's mindset.

You have learnt that you must possess or acquire the eight essential strengths in order to acquire a sufficient winner's mindset. You cannot over emphasise the importance of the essential strengths in respect to acquiring or strengthening that necessary mindset.

The driving strengths are those forces that assist in driving you to acquire the essential strengths.

As previously stated, the following are the eight (8) driving strengths:
- Drive;
- Proactivity;
- Motivation;
- Ambition;
- Willpower;
- Creativity;
- Intuition; and

- Curiosity.

Of the driving strengths, the first five, namely, drive, proactivity, motivation, ambition and willpower will ignite, fuel and launch your quest to attain the essential strengths. The next three, namely creativity, intuition and curiosity will significantly boost your drive.

If you do not already possess the driving strengths or any one or more of them, they are each capable of being acquired. If you already possess one or more of them, you may strengthen them.

As with the essential strengths, the process is to firstly identify which of the driving strengths you possess and the degree to which you possess them and, in doing so, to determine which driving strengths you do not possess and need to acquire.

Before undertaking the process, the next step is to obtain an understanding of the driving strengths in the context of a sufficient winner's mindset.

The driving strengths

The following is a brief explanation of each of the driving strengths:

1. Drive

In the context of the winner's mindset, drive is engendered by your passion to achieve your primary goal. It is activated by your singularity of purpose. It provides you with the unwavering motivation to keep going, step by step, until you achieve success.

When desire, determination and passion are underpinned by powerful drive, your tenacity for achieving your goal will know no bounds. It will manifest itself in the pursuit of your goal with resilience and stamina. It will not permit you to deviate from your purpose and will drive you to never quit until you achieve whatever your mind sets you to achieve.

You must have an unwavering singularity of purpose. You must drive yourself, never allowing yourself to be diverted from achieving your primary goal. Desire, determination, passion and positivity will give you that singularity of purpose.

At the first stage of developing a sufficient winner's mindset, you must determine your primary goal and once determined you must lay out your written plan on how you will achieve it. Once you have determined your primary goal, you must never allow yourself to be diverted from achieving it. Your drive takes over and step-by-step you will set about achieving your goal.

But, always remember that you are not infallible. You can and will make mistakes. You may set a goal, which for reasons beyond your control is, temporarily or permanently, unattainable. Circumstances may change. Whatever the reason, it is sometimes necessary to change or adapt your plan, goal or target. Life and circumstances do change. If so, you may need to adapt to those changing circumstances.

However, you must never allow your drive to lessen. You must never lose sight of your primary goal. It may sometimes be necessary to adapt your plan and maybe change your direction or approach in order to enhance your probability of achieving success. Regardless of any changes, never lessen your drive to attain your primary goal or any interim goal or target.

Far from being incompatible and depending upon changing circumstances, adaptability and drive may, at times, be an absolutely necessary combination.

2. Proactivity

Proactivity is a driving force that gets things done. Success will not come to you unless you make it happen.

You must be proactive in your approach. You must anticipate what must be done and do it decisively and without undue procrastination. You must stay ahead of events and not simply react to them after they have happened.

You must take the initiative to participate in and control events. You must play an active and not a passive role. You must try to accurately anticipate outcomes and prepare for likely consequences. You must think ahead and act proactively. You must make things happen. Being proactive is so important in managing the outcome and being a strong leader.

It does not mean blindly diving in without firstly anticipating the problems that you are likely to encounter.

Being proactive includes anticipating and thinking about problems you are likely to encounter in advance and how to best overcome them. On ascertaining what likely problems you will encounter you will be better equipped to overcome them when they arise and by being proactive you will take whatever steps are necessary, in advance, to prevent problems from occurring. Adaptable proactivity helps you to stay one step ahead of the game.

You do not wait for a problem to occur and then take action to overcome it. You must not be reactive, only reacting to problems after they have occurred. You must learn to anticipate problems and proactively deal with them.

You have already precisely defined your primary goal in writing, so you are absolutely clear what it is. You have already thought about and identified the obstacles that stand between you and the achievement of your goal. You have been proactive by thinking about and identifying the opportunities that will enable you to overcome those obstacles. You have prepared your written plan and determined its step-by-step implementation. By pre-planning, you started the whole process by being proactive.

It is an inherent part of proactivity to take whatever action is necessary to overcome anticipated problems. It's necessary to be proactive if you are to successfully achieve your plan. You must take the action and do the work necessary to achieve it in a positive decisive manner.

3. Motivation

Motivation is a force that is closely allied to drive. To see a motivated person driving forward and taking whatever action is necessary, never giving up until he or she succeeds is an inspiration to others.

Motivation is an intense inner feeling that drives you to achieve your goal. If you are strongly motivated you possess that driving force that enables you to take whatever risks are necessary to achieve it. It is what gets you out of bed each morning, raring to go.

You must be visionary in your thinking and highly optimistic about achieving your vision. You must invest endless physical, mental and emotional energy in your dedicated drive to achieve you goal. If motivated, you are hugely persistent and determined. If you temper your motivation, with a balanced approach, success will follow.

You must be truly motivated and never quit until you attain your goal. If so, you will be unstoppable!

4. Ambition

Ambition is a mental characteristic that drives you to better yourself and to achieve whatever it is that you want in life. It gives you the desire to gain whatever qualifications or special knowledge you may need to help fulfil your particular ambition.

It is the spring within the springboard that you will use to reach the very pinnacle of success in whatever it is that you strive for. It is one of the driving forces that will propel you to achieve success in your chosen field. It helps strengthen the foundation that underpins your desire to succeed and helps convert your dreams into reality. Ambition is a powerful driving force that drives you to develop your abilities and to achieve your goal.

If you posses ambition it will greatly assist you to acquire or strengthen your essential strengths. If, when you have undertaken your self-assessment and reality check, you decide that you are not ambitious or only ambitious to a limited degree, you should acquire or strengthen your ambition. Without ambition, you will not fully ignite the drive that you need.

However, be warned that whilst ambition is an important driving strength, if taken to the extreme, it could be harmful. Learn to balance your ambition. Over-ambition may cause you to run rough shod over others and this can be counter-productive. Your ambition is personal to you. Pursue it with all your might to emerge as a winner but do so in a way that does not intentionally hurt or offend others. Exercise your ambition carefully and in a manner that does not deliberately harm or sever relations with others or cause enmity. You never know when your paths may cross again in the future and you find yourself in the position of needing their support. In other words, be helpful to others where possible. Be respectful. Do not ride rough shod over others nor cause them intentional harm in the pursuit of your personal ambition.

Also, whilst nothing is impossible, try to avoid chasing what are seemingly unrealistic dreams. Maintain a reasonable balance wherever possible. Be single-minded and drive yourself to achieve your primary goal, but do so in a balanced manner. Be committed, but don't be manic in your approach.

Use your ambition to mobilise all your internal resources to help acquire or strengthen your essential strengths to reach your every goal and target.

5. Willpower

If you have willpower, you should possess control over your actions and thoughts. Control in the context of a sufficient winner's mindset relates to self-control and self-discipline.

Self-control is the control that you exercise over your actions. It prevents you from diverging from your plan or from being led astray. It gives you absolute steadfastness and singularity of purpose. It allows you to curb and exercise control over your excesses and emotional urges. It helps you to resist short-term temptations.

Self-discipline is the strength that results from the practice of exercising self-control over a prolonged period of time.

It makes self-control a habit. It is a state of mind that will drive you to perform all those tedious tasks that you must perform day after day, week after week, month after month over a long period of time until you successfully complete your plan. You should develop the habit of self-discipline and make it an integral part of your character. You must become a self-disciplined person.

Self-control and self-discipline are closely linked and, whilst different, they can sometimes be indistinguishable. They work in close harmony. Together, they constitute your willpower. You must possess strong willpower and, if you don't, you must develop or strengthen it. It is a powerful tool in helping you to develop your strengths.

It increases your capacity to be decisive and to act decisively. It helps you focus your energies on the task at hand. Willpower should be exercised in a rational balanced manner to avoid indulging in excessive behaviour that is likely to harm rather than help your progress.

Willpower will help you adhere to the long-term plan that you set yourself.

As part of a sufficient winner's mindset, it's necessary to have passion to the point that it is highly obsessive and intense. At the same time, your best results will be achieved by thinking and acting in a balanced rational manner. It is necessary therefore to control your passion to the extent necessary to ensure that it does not result in such excessive behaviour on your part that may prove to be harmful or counter productive. Willpower will help your maintain the necessary balance.

Willpower is the will to always do what you must do within the time period you set yourself. It will certainly assist you to acquire or strengthen your essential strengths.

Willpower will help you maintain the singularity of purpose that you must possess.

6. Creativity

If you possess inspired creative imagination, it could prove highly beneficial in various circumstances.

A creative imagination capable of identifying or creating opportunities with which to overcome obstacles that you encounter is a great asset. It will help you to develop solutions when formulating a written plan. Whilst it may not always be essential in developing or strengthening a sufficient winner's mindset, it is valuable when seeking solutions in order to overcome difficulties. An imaginative mind will help you seek out and find solutions and make decisions on how best to use them. By helping you discover imaginative solutions for problems you encounter, it often enhances your prospects of success.

Creative imagination will also assist you to develop your driving strengths, especially in developing imaginative ideas to help your drive and focus. By finding and doing what inspires you, you will more easily find creative imagination.

A person with a high level of creative imagination may sometimes be over imaginative and this could prove counter productive if, at times, it takes a person in too many directions. However, never discourage an overly imaginative mind. Simply learn to control it. Select and execute what you consider to be the best alternatives that your imagination conjures up for you.

7. Intuition

Intuition is a gut feeling or sixth sense, an instinct that gives you an apparent insight into the likely outcome of events in your life.

Depending on circumstances that arise and problems that you face, your mind processes information and unconsciously predicts the probable outcomes of events. You are unconscious of the process but cumulative knowledge that has resulted from past experience is stored in the recesses of your brain. As a result, you subconsciously develop a gut feeling or instinct for what is to come. Your brain processes information without you being aware of the process. You think unconsciously. As a result, you develop a hunch.

Unfortunately, gut feelings do not always lead to good decisions. In doing whatever is necessary to achieve your goal, there is no substitute for undertaking a full investigation and analysis of all relevant facts and their likely impact before making a decision.

In the context of a sufficient winner's mindset, an intuitive person, because of his or her visionary nature tends to be more inventive, possessing originality and being good and more inventive in solving problems that arise. It can prove to be a highly positive attribute when there is no apparent answer and you are left in doubt.

The best approach to adopt is to always make a full investigation of the relevant facts and their likely impact, before making a decision. But, if all else fails, go with your gut feeling.

8. Curiosity

If you are a curious person, you are inquisitive and possess a desire to discover, learn and acquire knowledge about matters that interest you.

You will find that curiosity and intelligence work hand-in-hand with each other. Intelligent people invariably possess a high level of curiosity.

If you are highly curious, your drive to discover new facts will intensify and as your knowledge increases, so will your capacity to develop new ideas. The danger is that if you are constantly thinking of new ideas, you may have difficulty in focusing. Always try to focus on developing and achieving one idea at a time. For this reason, both control and balance are important.

Curiosity is a strong asset through which to build and gather information. Keep looking for answers. Never stop questioning. It keeps your mind active, strengthening it and helping you to discover and be receptive to accepting new ideas. It adds a level of adventure and excitement to your day-to-day life and obliterates boredom.

Curiosity may be nurtured and developed. If you don't already possess it, you should acquire it. It is a very useful driving strength for anyone intent on acquiring or strengthening his or her essential strengths. This is especially so, if your curiosity is balanced and intelligently controlled.

In summary

The five driving strengths that play a key role in helping you to acquire and strengthen your essential strengths are drive, proactivity, motivation, ambition and willpower. The other three driving strengths are creativity, intuition and curiosity, all of which can play a powerful role in assisting you to acquire and strengthen drive and proactivity.

Drive and proactivity are the strongest keys to driving you to achieve the essential strengths. They cause you to take whatever action is necessary. Unless you take the necessary action wherever and whenever needed, little is achieved. Inactivity will get you nowhere.

Achieve a high level of drive and proactivity and you will already be well on the way to achieving and strengthening your essential strengths.

Drive, proactivity, motivation, ambition and willpower are also key elements in ensuring singularity of purpose. If there is one common essential thread to acquiring a sufficient winner's mindset and attaining your primary goal, it is singularity of purpose.

In conclusion

Please ensure that you understand all the driving strengths that you must acquire and how having them will help you.

By undertaking the self analysis process and the reality check process provided to you in Chapters 13 and 14, you will identify those driving strengths that you have, those that do not and those that you possess to a limited level and that need strengthening.

9
YOUR SUPPORTIVE STRENGTHS

> **Fundamental Principle Nine**
> Understand the supportive strengths that will assist you to gain the essential strengths, the driving strengths and a sufficient winner's mindset.

You have learnt that the winner's mindset is a state of mind that gives you the singularity of purpose to unwaveringly follow your plan every step of the way, never quitting until you achieve your primary goal. You have also learnt that you must possess those essential and driving strengths that you need in order to attain a sufficient winner's mindset.

You have learnt that there are eight driving strengths that will assist you to acquire those essential strengths that you do not possess and strengthen those that need strengthening.

In addition, there are eight supportive strengths, namely:
- Integrity;
- Reliability;
- Balance;
- Confidence;
- Optimism;
- Enthusiasm;

- Self reliance; and
- Adaptability.

Of the supportive strengths, integrity, reliability and balance cause others to trust and have confidence in you. Optimism, enthusiasm, confidence and self-reliance also have a positive effect on others. They see you as a buoyant and positive person. The last supportive strength, namely, adaptability, keeps you one step ahead of the constantly changing circumstances that you will encounter along your path.

If you do not already possess the supportive strengths or any one or more of them, they are each capable of being acquired. If you already possess one or more of them, you may strengthen them.

First, identify which of the supportive strengths you possess and the degree to which you possess them. In doing so, you will determine which supportive strengths you do not possess and need to acquire and which you possess to some extent, but which need strengthening.

Before undertaking the process of acquiring or strengthening them, your next step is to obtain an understanding of the supportive strengths in the context of the winner's mindset.

The supportive strengths

The following is a brief explanation of each of the supportive strengths:

1. Integrity

People with integrity are honest and have a strong sense of morality.

Like so many other character strengths, integrity is a characteristic that we should all possess. In business and in life generally and in your career, if you have integrity, you will be honest and will adhere to ethical conduct. With integrity, you will be fair in all dealings with others and, as a result will be regarded by others as trustworthy. In life, career and business, dishonesty never pays in the long term or at all. Honesty and fairness are the keys.

In life, career and business gaining the trust of others is highly important. Having a good reputation for being honest and trustworthy is gold. It will enhance your reputation and the reputation of your business. Customers or clients will want to deal with you and as a result you and your business will grow.

Would you rather take the short-term approach of earning a dishonest dollar and ruining your reputation or, would you rather embrace integrity and guarantee your long-term success?

There is no contest. The answer is obvious. Yet, there are so many dishonest people in this world, intent on taking unfair advantage at the expense of others.

Don't make the same mistake. Live your life honestly and with integrity. Unless you do, you will never achieve a sufficient winner's mindset. You will be driven by dishonesty, always chasing a quick dishonest dollar. Instead of having stability in life, career and business, instability will be your hallmark and others will not trust you.

If you do not already possess or act with integrity, it is something that must be acquired and applied in your personal life, career and business. It is simply a question of focusing on and ensuring that all your dealings with your clients, customers and others are conducted in a fair and honest manner.

If you sincerely concentrate on ensuring that all your dealings in your personal life, career and business are fair and honest and without duplicity of any nature whatsoever, you will quickly gain a business and personal reputation for always acting with scrupulous integrity and of being completely trustworthy.

It is just as easy to act with integrity as to act dishonestly. The long-term effects of always acting with integrity will far outweigh any short-term gains acquired by dishonest means. A reputation for integrity will grow your career and business and you will be trusted as a person. A reputation for dishonesty will destroy your career and business and, as a person, you will not be trusted.

The choice between integrity and dishonesty is a no brainer.

2. Reliability

If you are a reliable person, others will come to know that you are trustworthy and can be relied upon to do what you promise.

You do not commit lightly. You assess the position and if you commit to doing it, you stick to your commitment. Once you give your word, you abide by it. You do not give frivolous undertakings that you have no intention of carrying out. You mean what you say. You do not over promise and know when to say "No".

The traits you display include responsibility, stability and a strong sense of initiative, always working through and finishing what you start. You always try to do the right thing, often regardless of whether it goes against your own interests. Once you make a promise, you use best endeavours to keep it.

If you are not a reliable person, reliability is something you can and should train yourself to acquire. It's as easy as keeping your word. You must simply ensure that when you say you will do something, you do it.

Others always prefer to deal with a reliable person.

3. Balance

When you strive to achieve your primary goal and you do so with fierce determination and unswerving persistence until you achieve it, there can be a tendency to go to extremes. For that reason, you should balance your approach to avoid becoming manic. Whilst you must push yourself to your limits, day after day, until you achieve your goal, you should balance your actions. It takes a lot of hard work and time to achieve business success and unless you balance your approach and allow some time for relaxation, you run the risk of being less productive.

When creating a new business or undertaking or seeking to take an existing business or undertaking to the next level, putting in the necessary time and effort is essential to achieving the success you so fervently desire, but always ensure you take a balanced approach.

The advent of the computer has changed the way in which most of us work. In today's world, the computer has blurred the definitive line between your workplace and your home and has permitted work to intrude into the home. Depending upon the nature of your business, it may be possible to run your business entirely from home using your computer. In these cases, your workplace and your home become one and the same. If you work in an office or business away from your home, the computer allows you to also work from home outside your normal working hours in the office.

The computer has become so much an integral part of business, career and personal life, it's hard to imagine running a business, undertaking a job, obtaining information or communicating with friends, family, business associates or customers without one. At the same time, your computer makes you accessible to your employer, your employees, family, friends and customers 24/7.

The distinction between workplace and home has been blurred. For that reason, it's even more important to ensure that you achieve a balance between work and leisure time. Whilst it's important to relentlessly pursue your primary goal, it's also important to ensure that you take time off to relax.

The best way to achieve a healthy balance is to work to a plan that provides a necessary balance between work and relaxation. All work and no play, makes Jack a dull boy and Jill a dull girl.

Balance is not restricted to ensuring that you do not overwork. It is necessary in everything you do. Balance is always necessary to prevent you from overstepping the mark.

In the long term, achieving that healthy balance enhances your success in everything you do or attempt to do.

4. Confidence

You must possess an unshakeable self-confidence. You must have complete faith in yourself and your ability to successfully achieve your primary goal.

Self-confidence, self-esteem and self-belief come together as a united force that gives you that unshakeable sense that there is nothing you cannot achieve. Nothing is impossible. If you can conceive it, you are probably capable of achieving it. The self-belief in your skill and ability will empower you and boost your self-confidence.

In turn, it enhances the high regard you have for yourself. It makes you feel good about yourself as a person and that self-esteem positively engenders and enhances an assertive self-confidence in yourself and your abilities.

There are differences between self-belief and self-esteem. They are both important ingredients that will assist you to achieve and maintain a sufficient winner's mindset. But, whilst self-belief and self-esteem are important, when self-confidence is added, your mindset is substantially strengthened.

Self-belief is a belief in your own ability and skill. Self-confidence is gained by your accomplishment and experience. Self-esteem, namely the regard in which you hold yourself, is enhanced by achievement.

Let's also look at an example of how they work together.

Suppose you have the self-belief that you are the fastest runner in the world over a distance of one hundred metres. It's not until you win a gold medal at the Olympics for that event that you gain the absolute self-confidence that you are indeed the world's fastest runner over that distance. Confirmation takes your self-belief one step further and reinforces it. Self-esteem is how you feel about yourself. It's the positive regard that you have for yourself. It's your sense of self-worth. Whilst you believe yourself to be the world's fastest runner over a distance of one hundred metres, your self-belief gives you a high level of self-esteem. However, when you win that gold medal, you then know that you are the world's fastest. Your self-esteem is tremendously boosted. It is now based on belief and proven by accomplishment.

Self-belief and self-esteem are important ingredients of a sufficient winner's mindset but when you add self-confidence to the mix through accomplishment, your mindset is tremendously boosted in a positive manner.

Like other elements of the winner's mindset, self-confidence should be balanced. Ensure that you do not let yourself become over confident. Over confidence can lead to cockiness and arrogance. Attempting to acquire a sufficient winner's mindset with a cocky arrogant attitude will not succeed. Because of your attitude, others are far less likely to want to help or deal with you.

Self-belief, self-esteem and self-confidence are inner strengths. Keep them within. Let your actions speak for themselves. Others will recognise those characteristics in you and respect you for them. In dealing with others, remain humble. Never be cocky or arrogant.

Collectively, self-belief, self-esteem and self-confidence will help take you to the point, where for you, nothing is impossible.

Ensure that you do not let yourself become over confident. It leads to self-delusion. Stay balanced and let your results do the talking.

5. Optimism

Optimism is a positive mental attitude that causes you to anticipate and expect good outcomes in the future.

As an optimist you will have an inner faith that you will successfully achieve your primary goal and all interim goals and targets. As an optimist, you will have faith in the successful outcome of whatever you set out to achieve. It engenders a positive mindset and self-confidence.

Your future is full of promise. Your mind is filled with positivity and thoughts of a brighter future. You are less stressed and reduced stress levels are usually beneficial to your health. You expect a positive successful outcome regardless of the setbacks encountered on your way.

A positive optimistic attitude results in a higher level of success in life, career, business and whatever else you set out to achieve. Pessimism and self-doubt have the opposite effect and are not consistent with achieving a successful outcome.

The drive generated by a positive attitude also engenders persistence and a never say die attitude until your goal or target is achieved. Persistence contributes to optimists achieving a higher level of success. If at first you don't succeed, you keep trying until you do. You do not readily quit. Your mental attitude makes you more proactive and willing to take more calculated risks in your attempts to achieve your goal.

As an optimist your glass is always half full rather than half empty and every cloud has a silver lining. That positive attitude is a driving force that never accepts defeat or failure. For you, there are no failures but only setbacks from which to learn. Every setback is simply the result of a regrettable mistake. You readily admit your mistakes and are happy to learn from them and move forward expecting a successful outcome.

For you as an optimist, every setback has a positive result because you learn from every mistake and this creates a new opportunity to move forward. Every setback is a new start. It is your opportunity to learn and grow from the experience. You focus on the positive and not the negative. It is a platform from which to leap forward rather than stop or step backward.

Optimism is a positive healthy contagious attitude that engenders growth, never dwelling negatively on past setbacks. Every setback is a springboard from which to launch a fresh incentive. For you as an optimist, new opportunities abound.

Optimism is a strength that may be learned. You should possess it to a high level and, if you don't, you may acquire or strengthen it and abolish all pessimistic tendencies.

6. Enthusiasm

It must be an absolutely vehement enthusiasm to achieve your plan. It must be an eagerness that is so intense that it inspires, motivates and drives you. It also inspires and encourages others. It is contagious.

It engenders zeal within you, focusing your mind on what must be done. It motivates you. It creates an energy within you that drives and keeps you working your plan until you achieve it. It prevents you from quitting until you achieve a successful outcome. It breathes life into your thoughts, pushing you harder, driving you to convert your thoughts into reality.

Enthusiasm occupies your mind, consciously and subconsciously. In your day-to-day life, your enthusiasm for achieving your primary goal and each interim goal and target will not always be at the forefront of your conscious thought, but subconsciously it will always be there. It is a permanent part of your mindset, reinforcing your determination.

Enthusiasm and passion are closely related. They work in close harmony. One cannot exist without the other. Passion will intensify your enthusiasm and vice versa.

Enthusiasm is a great eagerness to do and follow through with your plan and convert your desire into reality. If you are really enthusiastic about what you want to achieve, you will push harder and keep pushing until you convert your desire into reality. Enthusiasm breathes life into your thoughts and readily converts them into action. Be enthusiastic in everything you do.

Enthusiasm is also infectious. It inspires others to follow your example and to apply the same zeal as they see in you. It is a great leadership asset.

7. Self-reliance

As a self-reliant person, you will rely on you own strengths and resources. You will trust yourself and your inner voices. You will be independent.

Your self-reliance compliments your intuition. Unlike intuition, which relies on your gut feeling, self-reliance is more about acting in a manner that your conscious thoughts dictate. It's about being an individual, following your beliefs and thoughts and not just blindly following society's norms or what is believed to be acceptable behaviour. It's about being independent, thinking for yourself and maintaining your independence in thought, word and action.

American philosopher, Ralph Waldo Emerson, warned us not to dismiss our personal insights or our gut feelings, simply because they originated within our imagination. Original thoughts are a powerful tool and we should give them full credence rather than dismiss them in favour of the thoughts of others, regardless of how eminent or well regarded that those others may be. Following your own inspiration and your own original thoughts often opens the door to great achievement. In this regard, be self-reliant.

At the same time remember what past experience has taught you. Let experience also be your guide.

Self-realisation is about self-trust. Not necessarily with blind faith, but certainly by seeing the merit in your thoughts or ideas. Follow and rely on yourself and your thoughts, rather than conform to the norm simply for the sake of conforming or because you're afraid to stick your neck out.

Believe in yourself. Be proud of your thoughts and ideas. Do not be afraid to express them or to argue their merits. Be nonconformist wherever and whenever you believe it is the better way to go.

8. Adaptability

Never underestimate the importance of adaptability. It will serve you well to acquire it as a strength.

In today's world, technology is advancing at such a rapid ever-increasing rate, that it's impossible to keep up unless you are adaptable. For business owners to take full advantage of the opportunities that are occurring as a result of those changes, adaptability is essential.

There are many aspects to adaptability. You need to be flexible and approach life, career and business with imagination. You cannot allow your mindset to be stuck in the rut of conformity. Instead, you must understand how the world has changed and continues to change. In order to take full advantage of the ever-changing business environment, you must take a different approach. You must be prepared to be nonconformist and keep an open mind, prepared to learn, to adapt and to seize new emerging opportunities and turn them to your business advantage. The same applies to your personal life and career. Versatility, not rigidity, must be your mantra.

You must be prepared to adjust and take advantage of the new opportunities that are rapidly changing the world in which you live. You must adapt your life and the way you do business to take advantage of every change that is positively beneficial.

If you don't change your approach and adapt, you will be left behind.

Adaptability is an important key.

In the context of achieving your primary goal, remember that circumstances change, new opportunities present themselves and other opportunities that once existed may no longer be available or viable. However, do not change your plan to attain your primary goal or any interim goal or target, unless, due to circumstances beyond your control, it becomes impractical. You have developed a plan through which to achieve your goal but if circumstances change or new opportunities arise, you must be prepared to alter or adapt your plan to the extent necessary to improve your chances of attaining your goal.

You must be open minded and adaptable and make whatever changes are reasonably necessary to successfully attain your goal even if it takes you outside your comfort zone. You must not make pre-conceived judgments.

Adaptability and unwavering drive are not incompatible. They compliment each other. It is simply a matter of timing and opportunity.

In summary

The supportive strengths are all those strengths that provide additional support to you when you are striving to attain an essential or driving strength to help reach your goal.

The three supportive strengths that cause others to have trust and confidence in you are integrity, reliability and balance. This trust and confidence is essential and will prove highly advantageous to your business, career and personal goals. That trust and confidence also has a highly positive effect in building your self-confidence and self-esteem.

This is enhanced when you add the supportive strengths of optimism, enthusiasm, confidence and self-reliance. They substantially further boost your sense of buoyancy and positivity.

The importance of the last supportive strength, namely adaptability, cannot be overstated. It keeps you ahead of the game, seeking new opportunities and allows you to adapt your plan where necessary to maximise those opportunities.

Please ensure that you understand all the supportive strengths that you should acquire and how having them will help you. If you do not already possess the supportive strengths that you need or any one or more of them, they are each capable of being acquired. If you already possess one or more of them, you may strengthen them.

Acquisition of the supportive strengths provides a huge boost to your overall abilities and your chance of achieving success.

In conclusion

Please ensure that you understand all the supportive strengths that you should acquire and how having them will help you.

By undertaking the self analysis process and the reality check process provided to you in Chapters 13 and 14, you will identify those supportive strengths that you have, those that do not and those that you possess to a limited level and that need strengthening.

10
YOUR ATTRIBUTES, TRAITS AND GOOD HEALTH

Fundamental Principle Ten
Understand the various leadership attributes, pleasant personality traits and the importance of good health, that will assist you to acquire a sufficient winner's mindset and successfully attain your every goal.

You have learnt that the winner's mindset is a state of mind that gives you the singularity of purpose to unwaveringly follow your plan every step of the way, never quitting until you achieve your primary goal. You have also learnt that you must possess and/or acquire the eight essential strengths to acquire the winner's mindset and that the eight driving strengths and the eight supportive strengths will greatly assist you to achieve all the essential strengths through which to acquire a sufficient winner's mindset

You have also learnt that there are five positive leadership attributes and four positive personality traits that could assist you and that good physical and mental health may prove essential attributes.

You have learnt that the five positive leadership attributes are:
- Strong leadership qualities;
- Hard work;
- Good communication;
- Organisational skills; and
- Intelligence.

You have learnt that the four positive personality traits are:
- A pleasant personality;
- Tact;
- Tolerance; and
- A good sense of humour.

You have learnt, in the context of a sufficient winner's mindset that good health includes good physical and mental health.

The primary goal that you have set for yourself is the goal that is most important to you and that you most want to achieve at that time. It is not the goal of some other person. Therefore you must be the driving force behind achieving it. No one else will achieve it for you. However, you do not live in isolation and you will probably need others to help you achieve your goal, especially if it is a business goal. As the driving force behind achieving your goal, you will be far more effective when seeking assistance from others if you are a strong leader that others respect. In this regard all five leadership attributes are important.

In addition to strong leadership attributes you will achieve far better cooperation from others if you have a pleasant personality. Others will respond more favourably to you if you lead by example in a pleasant manner rather than be autocratic and unpleasant.

Of course, serious physical or mental health issues will impair your ability to attain your goal, depending upon the nature and severity of your particular condition. Both good physical and mental health are highly conducive to the attainment of your goal.

Formula for Success in Life, Business and Career is not qualified to advise you on medical matters. If you have any reason to believe that you may suffer from any physical or mental health issue, you should consult your medical practitioner. In any event, whether you believe you have any health issues or not, it is advisable to have regular medical check ups. Better to be safe than sorry.

If you do not possess any or some of the leadership attributes or personality traits, they are each capable of being acquired. If you already possess one or more of them at an insufficient level, you may strengthen them.

As with the strengths, part of that process is to firstly identify which of the leadership attributes and personality traits you possess and, in doing so, determine which attributes or traits you do not possess and need to acquire or strengthen.

Have your doctor check your physical and mental condition and provide any medical treatment that may be necessary. Do not attempt to undertake the achievement of any goal or task without ensuring that it will not be detrimental to your health in any way.

Before undertaking the process, the next step is to obtain an understanding of both leadership attributes and personality traits in the context of the winner's mindset and the importance of good health.

Leadership attributes

The following is a brief explanation of each of the leadership attributes:

1. Leadership qualities

You must have or develop strong leadership qualities.

They give you the impetus to be the leader of the community or group that assists you in whatever you choose to do. As leader, you will be the front-runner and driver of whatever is achieved.

You must be the mentor of those who help support and follow you. As leader, you must lead by example, driving yourself to achieve your targets, never quitting until you succeed. You must incentivise your team by example and they will follow your lead, driving themselves to achieve their goals.

As the leader you must lead. You must not allow yourself to be diverted from single-mindedly following your plan until you achieve your primary goal. Being the leader prevents you from being diverted from your intentions. You must set an example to others always driving yourself to achieve your targets and showing others by example how to achieve theirs.

As a leader you must possess and be seen by others to possess self-confidence. You must inspire others, must display integrity and be accountable, never playing the blame game. The buck stops with you as the leader. You must accept responsibility for whatever happens under your watch. You must be committed to and passionate about achieving success. You must be prepared to delegate authority wherever necessary or appropriate and empower your delegate with all necessary authority. As a leader, you must be creative and exercise power with firmness but also show empathy towards and be supportive of your team.

Adding a pleasant personality to your other strong leadership qualities creates a stronger incentive in others to want to help, support and assist you to achieve your goal.

2. Hard work

A myth has been perpetrated that if you believe in something strongly enough, it will happen. The perpetrators of the myth tell you that if you wish for something fervently enough and believe strongly enough that you will receive it. They say that some imaginary force in the cosmos (or wherever) will make it happen. They tell you that if you want, say, $1,000,000 it will materialise in your bank account if you wish for it and believe with intense

10: Your Attritbutes, Traits and Good Health

strength that you will get the money. They say that this belief coupled with you undergoing a process of imagining yourself already in possession of the money will cause it to materialise. To achieve your desired result, they tell you that you must wholeheartedly immerse yourself in the belief that the money will be yours. If you do that, then Bingo, you will get $1,000,000. Things will miraculously happen and the money will flow to you and before you know it, there's $1,000,000 sitting in your bank account.

With all due respect, what a load of codswallop! What absolute nonsense!

Certainly, most people would like to win a major lottery. But, it doesn't matter how much you wish, believe or obsess about winning. Whether you win or not is entirely the luck of the draw. Every lottery has a winner or the lottery jackpots. Eventually someone will win the money. In fact many winners buy a ticket and never give it a second thought until they are told that they have won. It's simply the luck of the draw. Certainly some people seem to be luckier than others. However, you cannot rely on luck.

Luck may play a part in our lives, but to achieve a particular outcome we cannot rely on luck alone. In fact, we should not rely on it at all.

The desire to achieve a particular outcome coupled with a plan and the hard work necessary to execute it is what's necessary to achieve your primary goal. All the wishing, no matter how fervent, will get you nowhere unless coupled with a plan and the consistent hard work necessary to achieve it. Belief that you will achieve your goal may help keep you focused but will not in itself achieve it.

A plan and hard work will convert your dream into reality, provided that you have the singularity of purpose to see it through to a successful conclusion.

Don't wait for opportunities to come to you. Be proactive and create them. Work hard and successfully use them to your advantage.

3. Good communication

Good or effective communication means the communication of information to one or more persons in a manner that the meaning of what is communicated is clearly understood by the intended recipients.

In life, career and business, effective communication is highly important and beneficial. From a management perspective, its importance cannot be overstated.

It is a skill that may be readily acquired and should be. It is an essential skill for every business leader. An important and major part of that skill is the ability to simplify complex information in a manner that makes it easily understood by everyone. That ability is required for both written and verbal communication.

Effective listening is as important as effective speaking or writing. It's important to engage others by showing you are genuinely interested in their opinion or point of view.

Think carefully about the message you wish to convey. Make it concise, complete and to the point. Keep it relevant. Avoid ambiguity. Don't exaggerate. Use appropriate language. Make it persuasive. Maintain eye contact and smile.

Invite feedback. Wherever relevant, don't ignore the interests of the recipient, especially where the recipient stands to benefit.

4. Organisational skills

As an organised person, you will be methodical and well organised. You will preplan and follow your plan step-by-step in a systematic manner. You will be neat and tidy. You will file everything relevant and know where everything is kept.

As an organised person, you will keep everything under control, at your fingertips. You will work systematically to a plan. This usually makes you more efficient. You think everything through and carefully structure what must be done in advance in order to achieve your plan more efficiently. You prioritise what must be done in order of importance. You plan in advance. In turn, this makes you more productive.

As a planner, be aware of the watermelon principle. If the watermelon is too large to eat in one mouthful, cut it into small bite size pieces and eat it piece by piece until you have totally consumed it. In other words, as part of your plan, break down what must be done into smaller achievable tasks and complete them one by one until your goal is achieved. It's the same with acquiring or strengthening your strengths, attributes or traits. Acquire them systematically, one at a time. Strengthen them step-by-step and one at a time.

Everyone needs a planner on the team. Anyone can acquire the characteristics of being a meticulous planner. You should do what's necessary to acquire those skills. Every business needs meticulous planning and methodical execution of the plan. If for any reason you decide not to acquire those skills, you should engage a planner to assist you.

Always do your best, but never try to be a perfectionist.

5. Intelligence

Intelligence is an attribute that should never be underestimated. As an intelligent person, you probably possess a reasonably high degree of creative imagination and this results in an ability to think outside the square and create opportunities for yourself when needed. As a person with a high degree of intelligence, you will have the ability to more readily find solutions. You won't need to concentrate as much as a person without the same level of intelligence.

What is intelligence? According to the Oxford Dictionary, it is the ability to learn or understand things or to deal with difficult situations.

Everyone has intelligence. However, different people are born with different degrees and different types of intelligence. A practical person may pursue a natural ability to learn and understand various matters such as building or repairing motor vehicles, a mathematician may pursue a natural talent for solving complicated mathematical problems and a poet may pursue a natural facility for writing beautiful thought provoking poetry.

You would best know which form or forms of intelligence you possess. None of the above forms of intelligence make you more or less intelligent in the general sense. It's just that most of us are born with different forms of intelligence. As a result, we each have or develop a different bent. Of course there are some who are born with extraordinary intelligence. However, most of us posses average intelligence and it manifests itself in different ways for different people.

Regardless of whether you possess above average, average or below average intelligence, you should direct your intelligence to help achieve your primary goal. It is possible to boost and increase your intelligence level. Always work on doing so.

Be warned however that being gifted with an exceptionally high degree of intelligence could also be a disadvantage because as an exceptionally intelligent person, you do not require the same degree of concentration or hard work as someone with less intelligence. If something comes too easily, you can become lazy.

Intelligence, concentration and hard work come together as an unbeatable combination and help you to achieve your primary goal and every other interim goal or target.

Positive personality traits

The following is a brief explanation of each of the pleasant personality traits:

1. A pleasant personality

It is important to create a good impression with others and in order to achieve this, having a pleasant personality is highly beneficial.

Others respond favourably to you if you have a pleasant personality. The manner in which you treat others will usually result in the manner in which they treat or respond to you.

When you pursue your goal, you will probably often require the help and goodwill of others. A pleasant personality will help you to more easily make friends and, as a result, more easily gain the support you need from others.

If you don't already possess a pleasant personality, it's relatively easy to develop one providing you are able to exercise self-control. Remember that self-control is also a characteristic that may be acquired.

You should exercise and direct your self-control in a manner that enables you to quickly acquire a pleasant personality and use it when dealing with others.

A pleasant personality is made up of many different characteristics and the personality traits that attract one person to another differs from person to person and to that extent, it can be highly subjective.

However, generally speaking, the traits of a pleasant personality include an extensive variety of traits such as balance, compassion, control, enthusiasm, courtesy, an even-tempered disposition, a sense of fair play, friendliness, a fun loving attitude, genuineness, respect for others, being a good listener and having a great sense of humour.

You might like to add any other relevant traits to the above list that appeal to you.

Remember, the first impression you make on others is created by various factors including the clothes you wear and your general appearance, what you say and how you say it. The first impression you create, although it may be relatively superficial, is nevertheless highly important.

First impressions tend to last, as do general opinions that others will form about you, based on first impression.

So, always ensure that you are well presented and be careful with what you say and how you say it. Always ensure that you not only make a good first impression, but that you continue to act in a manner that will enhance your first impression.

2. Tact

A person with tact is sensitive to the feelings, thoughts, beliefs, ideas and opinions of others and is courteous when talking or otherwise communicating with them.

Before communicating, you should think about the response of the other person. Try to ensure that the response is likely to be appropriate and relevant. Try to say whatever will help engender a response that positively advances the conversation in an appropriate non-aggressive manner.

At the outset of every conversation, think in advance and ensure that what you say is likely to engender a friendly positive response from others.

When you are involved in written communication, this is more easily done because you have time to think. When in oral conversation however, you have far less time, so extra care is needed. One approach is to always soften your response by offering an explanation of your opinion in advance to ensure that it is understood in its proper context. Whenever engaging in oral communication, exercise good judgment and do not say anything if you believe it may offend. Your response should never be intentionally offensive.

Always take a diplomatic approach and avoid being too opinionated or intentionally offensive. This should not prevent you from stating your point of view, but when you do, ensure that you are respectful. Understand that everyone is entitled to an opinion. State your opinion in a calm, reasoned, non-argumentative manner. Present your opinion as another way to look at a situation rather than adopting an attitude of it's my way or the highway.

Tact is a virtue that can be acquired. If you acquire tact it will prove extremely valuable in life, career, business and whatever else you set out to achieve. It is a great foundation on which to establish the basis for effective communication and for good effective negotiation. It is the ability to deliver difficult messages in a way that considers other people's feelings and preserves relationships.

3. Tolerance

As a tolerant person, you accept and show understanding towards the beliefs and practices of others no matter how much you may be opposed to, dislike or disagree with them.

You should believe that everyone is entitled to their own opinion and be afforded the opportunity to express and follow their beliefs. You do not force your opinions on others. You endeavour to understand where the other person is coming from.

You listen carefully to the opinions of others whether you agree with them or not. Your response is not hateful or arrogant. You try to always be agreeable and to treat others with dignity and respect, tolerating their views.

As a tolerant person, you are able to recognise, distinguish and appreciate the difference between opinion and fact. It is a great advantage. You should never confuse opinion with fact. Unfortunately a major trait of intolerant people is that they present their opinions as facts. Many of them are so self opinionated that they are convinced that their opinions are fact. Opinionated self-righteousness breeds intolerance.

Tolerance breeds patience. It allows constructive debate.

It avoids argument and allows a free exchange of ideas. It is inoffensive. It helps build good friendly relations with others. It shows respect. It removes animosity.

Like tact, tolerance is a virtue than may also be acquired. If you are not a tolerant person, you should acquire tolerance. It will prove highly valuable in life, career, business and every other pursuit.

Tolerance is a great way of developing friendly relations with others.

4. A good sense of humour

If you have GSOH or a good sense of humour, you have the ability to appreciate the funny side of things, to understand and laugh at jokes. And usually, you have the capacity to laugh at yourself.

There is a difference between having a sense of humour and being funny. Both can be important in life, career and business. Being funny is of course having the ability to make others laugh, whereas having a sense of humour is having the ability to appreciate humour. People who are funny have a sense of humour. People with a sense of humour are not necessarily naturally funny.

You must learn to take a joke. Avoid making jokes at the expense of others or that are inappropriate, in bad taste, or likely to give offence. If you offend, apologise sincerely and in good grace.

If you have a good sense of humour, you are probably a more creative person. You tend to be more spontaneous and accepting and to more readily take things in your stride. As an intelligent person, you tend to have a good sense of humour. You tend to look at the brighter side of life and are therefore more optimistic.

You usually have a greater ability to make friends and to draw others into assisting you with your endeavours. As a result, it helps your leadership abilities.

A good sense of humour and being funny can prove a great asset. People are usually born with the capacity to be funny, but you can develop and strengthen a strong sense of humour.

Think about it carefully. It is a great advantage to have GSOH.

Good health

Apart from your strengths, attributes and positive personality traits, you should never underestimate the importance of maintaining good health. The lack of good health may prevent you from achieving your primary goal, interim goals and targets.

Good health may be divided into two categories, namely good physical health and good mental health. Both must be maintained.

The lack of good health may or may not have been caused by factors under your control. For example, you may have a genetic disposition to a particular medical condition or your medical condition may have been caused by an illness transmitted to you in circumstances beyond your control. On the other hand, it may have been caused by factors entirely under your control.

You may be suffering from ill health due to a long period of self-indulgence. For example, smoking cigarettes or the excessive consumption of recreational drugs or alcohol. These people usually have little self-control, do not possess willpower and have a tendency to make excuses and procrastinate. Whether smoking cigarettes, taking recreational drugs or drinking alcohol, their addictive nature is difficult to overcome and to kick any of those habits strong willpower is necessary.

Regardless of the underlying cause of your medical condition and whether it was self-inflicted or not, severe ill health is one factor that could prevent you from following your plan and less severe bouts of ill health will often inhibit your ability to pursue a goal or target, if even on a temporary basis. Maintaining good physical and mental health is essential.

For example, suppose, after smoking for several years, you suffer from severe emphysema. As a result, you are bedridden in hospital and connected to an artificial lung to facilitate your breathing. It would be impossible under those circumstances to achieve most physical goals.

The maintenance of good mental and physical health can be and is often essential to ensure that you are capable of following your plan to a successful conclusion and attaining your goal.

Always be conscious of the importance of good health and exercise self-control to ensure that you live a healthy lifestyle. Completely avoid taking recreational drugs and smoking and avoid drinking to excess. Maintain a healthy diet. Exercise. Stay fit and healthy and have periodic medical checks to detect symptoms of any illness or condition that might adversely affect your physical or mental health.

Good health can be essential to your ability to achieve your primary goal and your every interim goal and target.

In summary

Leadership qualities, attributes and traits will assist you to attain your goal and will also prove to be especially helpful when it comes to gaining assistance from others to help you do so.

This is achieved by displaying strong leadership qualities including leadership by example through hard work, good communication and organisational skills, all applied with intelligence and integrity. Display those characteristics and others will look up to you and follow your example.

When you add a pleasant personality, tact, tolerance and GSOH, others will enjoy working with you and your team of helpers will grow.

If you do not already possess those attributes or traits or any one or more of them, they are each capable of being acquired. If you already possess one or more of them, you may strengthen them.

Acquisition of the attributes and traits and the addition of good physical and mental health will greatly boost your overall abilities and your chances of success.

In conclusion

Please ensure that you understand the importance of leadership attributes, pleasant personality traits and good health.

By undertaking the self analysis process and the reality check process provided to you in Chapters 13 and 14, you will identify those attributes and traits that you have, those that you do not and those that you possess to a limited level and that need strengthening.

You should periodically consult a medical practitioner and ensure that you remain in good physical and mental health.

11
YOUR WEAKNESSES

Fundamental Principle Eleven
Identify and understand your weaknesses that will prevent you from acquiring a sufficient winner's mindset and your goals.

The weaknesses that prevent you from acquiring a sufficient winner's mindset are the opposite of the various strengths, attributes and traits that assist you to achieve it.

You should identify and recognise your weaknesses. Be aware of them and of any tendency you may have towards any particular weakness or weaknesses. It helps to know what your particular weaknesses and harmful tendencies are. You cannot overcome or avoid them if you do know what they are.

Whatever your assessment may be, always remember that overcoming a weakness or harmful tendency is as simple as acquiring its corresponding strength, attribute or positive trait. For example, if you have a tendency to be negative, you overcome it by acquiring the strength of positivity. By acquiring positivity, you eradicate negativity.

It is unnecessary to overly dwell on weaknesses in this book. We prefer to dwell on strengths, attributes and positive traits.

For that reason, this chapter simply identifies and provides a brief description of each weakness that is the opposite of each of the essential, driving and supportive strengths, the leadership attributes and positive personality traits.

Gain the requisite strengths, attributes or positive traits and you will automatically eradicate their corresponding weaknesses.

Essential strengths and corresponding weaknesses

The essential strengths and their corresponding weaknesses are:

Desire:	Apathy;
Determination:	Aimlessness;
Passion:	Indifference;
Positivity:	Negativity;
Focus:	Inattentiveness;
Persistence:	Fickleness;
Commitment:	Non-commitment; and
Decisiveness:	Indecisiveness.

Those corresponding weaknesses are briefly explained as follows:

Apathy

If you are apathetic you will be indifferent towards achieving your goal. As a result you will not have the level of desire that is necessary to drive you to achieve it. Instead you will display a lack of interest.

Aimlessness

If you are aimless, your mind will drift aimlessly from one idea to the next. You will be unable to focus on achieving your goal.

You will be incapable of having the determination you need to relentlessly pursue your goal until you successfully achieve it.

Indifference

If you are indifferent towards achieving your goal, you will not have the passion to pursue it. Passion is the spark that ignites your drive. Indifference extinguishes that spark.

Negativity

If you are a negative person, you will always find a reason why you will not achieve your goal or why you will fail. Negative thinking is harmful and destructive. You cannot on the one hand be negative about achieving your goal whilst simultaneously expecting to achieve a positive result. Negativity breeds doubt. As a result, it destroys the drive you require and sets you up for failure.

Inattentiveness

If you are inattentive, you lack the ability to pay attention or to concentrate. Your mind will wander aimlessly and you will not focus on the tasks that you must perform to achieve your goal. Without the ability to focus your thoughts and efforts, you will not succeed.

Fickleness

If you have a fickle mind, you will be aimless and inattentive and, as a result, you will lack consistency of purpose. Without consistency of purpose you cannot maintain the persistent drive necessary to achieve your goal.

Non-commitment

If you are not committed to achieving your goal, you will not achieve it, especially if it is a long-term goal. If you are not committed you will not have the persistent drive that is necessary.

Indecisiveness

If you are indecisive, you will be irresolute, unable to decide on which course of action to take. This will induce doubt. Doubt in yourself or your plan will weaken your resolve to achieve your goal. It will cause you to procrastinate instead of decisively taking the necessary action.

Driving strengths and corresponding weaknesses

The driving strengths and their corresponding weaknesses are:

Drive:	Lethargy;
Proactivity:	Inactivity;
Motivation:	Demotivation;
Ambition:	Ambitionless;
Willpower:	Weak willed;
Creativity:	Non-creativity;
Intuition:	Non-intuitive; and
Curiosity:	Disinterest.

Those corresponding weaknesses are briefly explained as follows:

Lethargy

If you are lethargic, you will be idle and inactive and disinclined towards pursuing your goal. You will lack the necessary energy and drive to pursue it and your sluggishness and laziness will induce you to become unresponsive.

Inactivity

If you are inactive or reactive, you will not be proactive. Your inactivity will prevent you from taking timely action and will cause you to do nothing and then react to the situation, often too late. Neither is it conducive to you taking action to forestall or overcome obstacles that you are likely to encounter.

Demotivation

If you are demotivated, you will not have the motivation to pursue your goal. Instead you will have no enthusiasm and will lack interest in pursuing it to a successful conclusion. Without motivation little, if anything, will be achieved.

Ambitionless

If you are devoid of ambition, you will have little, if any, desire to succeed in the achievement of your goal or anything else that might take your fancy or in any way advance you to a higher level of achievement. You will be aimless and not driven to attain a goal or fulfil any ambition in life. You will remain content with whatever life doles out to you.

Weak willed

If you are weak willed, you will lack self-control. You will have little control, if any, over rashness, recklessness or intemperance. You will lack strength of character. In the context of a sufficient winner's mindset, you will lack the self-control necessary to maintain the singularity of purpose that is necessary to achieve your goal.

Non-creativity

If you are non-creative, you will lack the resourcefulness of mind that allows you to create opportunities with which to overcome obstacles that you encounter. A dull uncreative non-innovative mind is not inspirational and is not conducive to developing imaginative solutions when required.

Non-intuitive

If you are not intuitive, you will lack the intuition or the gut feeling that provides a possible solution to any problem you face. Whilst intuition may prove useful, always remember that it is based on your gut feeling and not upon conscious reasoning and may not be reliable.

Disinterest

If you are not interested in the attainment of your goal, you will not be personally involved or driven to attain it. You will not achieve a goal unless you have that personal interest, desire and drive.

Supportive strengths and corresponding weaknesses

The supportive strengths and their corresponding weaknesses are:

Integrity:	Dishonesty;
Reliability:	Unreliability;
Balance:	Imbalance;
Confidence:	Non-confidence;
Optimism:	Pessimism;
Enthusiasm:	Unenthusiasm;
Self reliance:	Dependence; and
Adaptability:	Inflexibility.

Those corresponding weaknesses are briefly explained as follows:

Dishonesty

If you are a dishonest person, you will not conduct yourself with integrity. If you are dishonest in business or your personal life, others will not trust you. Without the trust of others you cannot build a successful long-term business or personal relationships.

Unreliability

If you are unreliable, you consistently fail to keep your promises. You are inconsistent and probably undisciplined. You are not a person of your word and others will soon learn that you cannot be relied upon. To succeed in the long term, your word must be your bond. Having a reputation for unreliability is destructive.

Imbalance

If there is an imbalance between your personal, career and business life, or if you manage your time in life, career, business or anything else in an unbalanced or erratic fashion, it will have a negative and disruptive effect on you and whatever you seek to achieve. Avoid imbalance and work within the most conducive balanced environment that you are able to achieve.

Non-confidence

If you are uncertain, you will engender doubt and lose self-confidence. You will be unsure of yourself and your abilities. Once doubt seizes your mind, you are on a downward slope to failure. You must abolish uncertainty and stay positive regardless of the obstacles you face.

Pessimism

If you are pessimistic, you will allow doubt to dominate your thoughts. You cannot be optimistic if you doubt that you will achieve your goal. Pessimism is an insidious invasion of your mind born of uncertainty. Abolish it. Pessimism is not conducive to success and, if strong enough, will prevent you from being successful.

Unenthusiasm

If you are unenthusiastic, you don't care one way or the other whether you achieve your goal or not. There is no passion on your part, no determination, no desire and no commitment. Enthusiasm leads to success. Unenthusiasm lays the seeds of failure.

Dependence

If you are overly dependent on others, you will display traits that you are not independent or self- reliant. You must rely on others to a certain extent. Over dependence on others to the point where you unnecessarily depend on them is what you must guard against. Self-reliance and self-belief boost your chances of success.

Inflexibility

If you are completely inflexible in the face of changing circumstances that demand change, you will fail. Flexibility and adaptability are essential on your path to success. Common sense and circumstances dictate what changes should be made. Remove inflexibility and be adaptable wherever it helps you to succeed.

Leadership attributes and corresponding weaknesses

Leadership attributes and their corresponding weaknesses are:

Leadership qualities:	Ineffective leadership;
Good communication:	Ineffective communication;
Organisational skills:	Disorganisation;
Hard work:	Laziness; and
Intelligence:	Unintelligence.

Those corresponding weaknesses are briefly explained as follows:

Ineffective leadership

If you have an inflated ego, if you are autocratic, if you do not lead whether by example or otherwise, if you are inconsistent, if you do not accept responsibility for your actions or if you always blame others for everything that goes wrong, you will be an ineffective leader. Others will not respect or readily follow and support you.

Ineffective communication

If you are unable to clearly and concisely communicate your instructions or requirements to others, you lack one of the fundamental requirements of leadership. A leader must learn the art of clear effective communication that is unlikely to be misunderstood or misinterpreted.

Disorganisation

If you are unable to properly plan, efficiently organise and exercise effective control over your activities, you lack one of the essential leadership qualities. You cannot be disorganised in the way you work or have a disorganised mind.

Laziness

If you are lazy, you will be an ineffective leader. You must lead by example. You cannot expect members of your team to work hard at their allocated task unless you lead by example. By working hard and going the extra mile whenever needed, you lead by example and encourage others to follow your lead. A good leader must never be lazy or be seen to be lazy.

Unintelligence

If you are unintelligent, you will not have the capacity to consistently make the right decisions. Intelligent leadership builds confidence in others. If as a leader, you make the right decision most of the time and quickly rectify any wrong decision that you may have made, you will be viewed as intelligent. There is no place for unintelligent leadership.

Pleasant personality traits and corresponding weaknesses

The pleasant personality traits and their corresponding weaknesses are:

Pleasant personality:	Unpleasant personality;
Tact:	Tactlessness;
Tolerance:	Intolerance; and
Good sense of humour:	Humourless.

Those corresponding weaknesses are briefly explained as follows:

Unpleasant personality

If you are narcissistic, arrogant, aggressive, a bully, possess an inflated ego or are intolerant of the views of others, you possess an unpleasant personality. You will be disliked. You will not have many, if any, friends. You will not enjoy the loyalty and support of others. You will not fit easily in the business or social world.

Tactlessness

If you are blunt, inconsiderate, thoughtless, or undiplomatic you are a tactless person and are prone to offending others. Tactless people are usually selfish and self-centered. They often fail to display empathy. In career, business and personal life, where the support of others is required, tactlessness will usually be counter-productive.

Intolerance

If you are unwilling or unable to accept the views of others, especially when they differ from yours, you are intolerant. You will have an attitude of it's my way or the highway. Others will not tolerate or accept your intolerance. Where the support of others is required, intolerance will not gain you that support.

Humourless

If you are overly serious about everything and do not appreciate humour, you are probably humourless. You tend to be inflexible and don't appreciate others displaying humour or joking around. Humour is useful in breaking down conflict or tension and it helps you to make friends more easily. If you do not possess GSOH you are lacking a highly important attribute.

Good health and its corresponding weakness

Lastly we deal with the positive aspects of good physical and mental health and their corresponding weaknesses:

    Physical good health: Physical ill health; and
    Mental good health: Mental ill health.

The corresponding weaknesses are briefly explained as follows:

Physical ill health

There are many varieties of physical ill health. In the context of the winner's mindset and the achievement of goals, physical ill health is relevant when its physical effect is so serious that it prevents you from achieving your goal regardless of whether you have a sufficient winner's mindset or not. It is where your physical ill health deteriorates to the extent that it prevents or seriously affects your physical ability to achieve your goal.

Mental ill health

There are also many varieties of mental ill health. In the context of a sufficient winner's mindset and the achievement of goals, mental ill health is relevant when its effect is so serious that it prevents you from acquiring the necessary mindset or achieving your goal because you do not have the mental capacity to do so. It is where your mental ill health deteriorates to the extent that it seriously affects your mental ability to achieve your goal.

There is nothing to be done other than to seek the necessary medical treatment to remedy any illness, whether physical or mental and to restore your good health.

In summary

Weaknesses seriously impair your ability to attaining your primary goal and every interim goal and target.

The most dangerous weaknesses are those that counteract the essential strengths. They are apathy, aimlessness, indifference, negativity, inattentiveness, fickleness, non-commitment and indecisiveness.

However, it should always be remembered that all the other weaknesses are or can be dangerous and should all be eliminated if relevant in that they prevent you from achieving your goal. As previously stated, the process of eliminating a weakness is to acquire its corresponding positive strength, attribute or trait. By acquiring it, you will automatically eliminate the weakness.

In conclusion

Please ensure that you identify all your weaknesses and understand the importance of eradicating them.

By undertaking the self-analysis and the reality check processes provided in Chapters 13 and 14, you will identify those weaknesses that you have. Once you have identified that they are preventing you from attaining your particular primary goal, interim goal or target, you should do whatever is necessary to eliminate them.

In the case of ill health, whether mental or physical, you should consult a medical practitioner.

12
ACQUIRING YOUR SUFFICIENT WINNER'S MINDSET

> **Fundamental Principle Twelve**
> Identify each mindset strength, attribute or trait that you do not possess or do not possess to a sufficient degree and which is preventing you from successfully attaining a sufficient winner's mindset. Acquire or strengthen each such strength, attribute or trait as may be necessary. Do not quit until you attain a sufficient mindset.

The process for acquiring a sufficient winner's mindset is a process of acquiring those mindset strengths, attributes and positive personality traits that you do not possess and strengthening those that you do to a sufficient extent to ensure that you acquire and maintain the necessary mindset. Overcoming material obstacles is not relevant here, only mindset obstacles.

A sufficient winner's mindset in the context of this book means a mindset that contains the strengths, attributes and positive personality traits to a sufficiently strong degree to enable you to attain your primary goal and each and every interim goal or target along the way. Not every strength, attribute or trait must necessarily be acquired or strengthened. It varies from person to person and depends on the particular goal and particular circumstances of each person. Only identify those strengths, attributes and traits that are needed to achieve your particular goal or target at that time and disregard those that are not.

You have already defined and are aware of your primary goal. You are already aware that in order to achieve your primary goal there will be a step-by-step process that you must follow to achieve it. You are aware that those steps include achieving interim goals and targets along the way and that the achievement of those interim goals and targets may also be a step-by-step process.

You should understand that achieving a sufficient winner's mindset is a necessary requirement for achieving your primary goal and each interim goal and target. To that extent, achieving a sufficient winner's mindset is, in itself, an essential interim goal. It is not your primary goal. It is a necessary step towards the achievement of your primary goal.

You have already commenced and partly completed the process of identifying the particular mindset strengths, attributes and traits that you must possess or strengthen in order to achieve a sufficient mindset. You did this when you answered your Exercises. You will complete the process when you answer the self-analysis questions in Chapter 13 and have someone complete the answers to the reality check questions in Chapter 14.

Your mindset obstacles that prevent you from achieving your interim goal of attaining a sufficient winner's mindset are the lack of the mindset strengths, attributes and traits that you have identified or that you lack to a significant degree. By acquiring or strengthening them, you overcome those mindset obstacles. The guidelines provided later in this chapter will enable you to acquire the sufficient winner's mindset that you need.

Before undertaking your identification and assessment process, you should understand that it is not always necessary to acquire or strengthen every strength, attribute and trait of a winner's mindset. It is only necessary or important to attain a sufficient winner's mindset by acquiring or strengthening those that are necessary to achieve your particular goal or target. For example: Suppose you are a sole trader who works alone, without any staff, in the business of purchasing mechanical tools from manufacturers and wholesaling them to retailers in your area. Your goal is to be highly successful in your business and each year you target a high minimum annual profit to be earned by your business. In that example, it would be unimportant if you lacked leadership qualities as an attribute because you are a sole trader. In fact, they are irrelevant. On the other hand, a sufficient willpower would probably prove to be highly significant to keep you on track.

Further, in assessing the degree to which you must possess a strength, attribute or trait, a score of "7" or above is considered acceptable in all cases where the acquisition of a particular strength, attribute or trait is necessary or important. However in cases such as in the example above, where a particular strength, attribute or trait is neither essential nor important, the score you achieve is also irrelevant. It does not matter in such cases, how high or low your score may be.

When pursuing a sufficient winner's mindset, only seek to strengthen those elements of the winner's mindset that are essential or important and are needed to ensure that you attain you goal or target.

Always remember, when acquiring a sufficient winner's mindset, firstly identify what, in your case, are the strengths, attributes and/or traits that are necessary or important for you to achieve or strengthen and then let nothing stop you from achieving or strengthening them.

That step-by-step process for acquiring your sufficient winner's mindset is set out below.

Acquiring a sufficient winner's mindset

Step 1

Identify your relevant mindset obstacles. Do this by comparing each answer you gave in your self-analysis in relation to a strength, attribute and trait in Chapter 13 with each answer you received in the reality check process provided in Chapter 14 for the same strength, attribute or trait. Do the comparison one answer at a time.

In both the self-analysis and the reality check process, there are two questions asked in relation to each strength, attribute and trait. Firstly compare the answer to the question that calls for a "Yes" or "No" answer. Secondly compare the answer to the question that asks for a score in order to assess the degree to which you possess a particular strength, attribute or trait on a scale of 0 to 10.

Suppose for example in the question which asks whether you possess integrity as a character strength, the answer given in both the self-analysis and the reality check is "Yes" and in the question asking for a score to determine the degree to which you possess integrity, the answer given in both the self-analysis and the reality check is "7". In this example, there is no disagreement as to your integrity and you should accept those answers as final.

Using another example, suppose in the question that asks whether you possess positivity, the answer given in the self-analysis is "Yes" and the answer in the reality check is "No". Which is correct? You must decide by thoroughly and honestly assessing both answers and making a choice. You must personally make the final choice. No other person should do that for you. However, as part of the process of making that final decision you

12: Acquiring Your Sufficient Winner's Mindset

must consider the answer given in the reality check and take it into account if you believe the answer may be credible.

If the answer given in the self-analysis as to whether you possess positivity is "Yes", it follows that you must provide a score for the degree to which you consider you possess it. Suppose that you have given yourself a score of "5 in" your self-analysis. At the same time, if in the reality check, the answer as to whether you possess positivity is "No", it follows that the score in your reality check must be zero. Which is correct — zero or "5"? You must assess the answers and decide. If you alter your self-analysis answer to "No", then clearly you must adjust your score to zero. However if you consider that you do possess a degree of positivity and stay with your original self-analysis answer, you must then decide whether you stay with your original score of "5" or reduce it.

On the other hand, suppose the answer in your reality check as to whether you possess positivity was "Yes" and the score given in the reality check was higher than the score of "5" that you gave in your self-analysis, you would need to consider whether you should adjust your self-analysis score by increasing it.

If you have been honest in providing your self analysis answers and the person who answers the reality check questions knows you well and answers honestly, the probability is that your self analysis answers and the reality check answers of "Yes" or "No" are more likely to be the same. However, it is less probable that the score given by you in your self-analysis will be the same as the reality check score because you and the other person are making a separate independent estimate in a scenario where the odds against them being the same are 1 in 10.

In all cases where there is a discrepancy between an answer in the self-analysis and an answer in the reality check in relation to the same strength, attribute or trait, you must, as explained in the example, consider the difference in the answers and make whatever changes, if any, you believe are required by adjusting your self-analysis answer.

If you are in doubt, you should always give the benefit of the doubt to the person who gave the reality check answer and adopt that decision. When making an assessment of the other person's answer, you should ask him or her to explain the reason or reasons underlying the answer. However, this must never be done before the final answer has been completed in writing by that person and you must never argue with the other person about the answer or make any attempt to influence that person to change it. Based on the reasons given, you must use best endeavours to assess which is the right answer. In doing so, forget your ego. Ego sometimes gets in the way of admitting your deficiencies.

Remember, for a sufficient winner's mindset, identify which of the strengths, attributes and traits are essential or important and concentrate on them. Ignore those that are not.

Unless time is of the essence, it is more important to acquire or strengthen your strength, attribute or trait than to acquire it within a particular time. However, if time is of the essence, you must try and set yourself an accurate time limit and acquire what you are seeking within the relevant time period.

Make your comparisons step-by-step and one at a time in the same order as they appear in the questions contained in Chapters 13 and 14.

Step 2

When you have completed Step 1, use one or more A4 sheets of paper, as necessary, and draw a vertical line down the middle of each sheet. Head the left column as "Strengths, Attributes and Traits to be Acquired or Strengthened" and the right column as "Score".

Based upon your comparisons and your decisions made under Step 1, write each strength, attribute and trait that you

12: Acquiring Your Sufficient Winner's Mindset

now consider that you either lack completely or that you have scored at "6" or less. Ignore those to which you have given a final score of "7" or more. Write the strength, attribute or trait in the left column and its score on the same line in the right column. You will recognise those strengths, attributes and traits that you consider are completely lacking, by the zero score.

Understand that your process is to obtain a sufficient winner's mindset and for this you only need to acquire those strengths, attributes or traits that are sufficient for that purpose depending upon the goal or target you are seeking to achieve.

If necessary, go back to the explanation in the early part of this chapter and remember that you may not necessarily need to acquire every strength, attribute and trait, but only those that are necessary or important in assisting you to achieve your particular goal. To assist you, it may be helpful to reread the example given of the sole trader.

Carefully reconsider the list that you have made and whether or not each strength, attribute and trait listed is necessary or important in assisting you to acquire or strengthen your particular goal or target. If not, delete it. Repeat this process for each strength, attribute or trait that you have listed in relation to each particular goal or target.

Step 3

In the process of acquiring a sufficient winner's mindset, you have completed Step 2 and should now be aware of each strength, attribute and trait that you require at a sufficiently high level in respect to each goal and target. You must acquire them one at a time.

In the process of acquiring each strength, attribute or trait and maintaining it at a sufficiently high level, you must firstly consciously decide that you will acquire it and, where necessary, strengthen that particular strength, attribute or trait. You must make that decision and constantly remind yourself of it and why it's important. In doing so, you condition your mind.

Suppose you wish to acquire or strengthen "integrity". Ensure that you understand what it means. The Oxford Dictionary describes it as the quality of being honest and having strong moral principles.

In order to have integrity, you must firstly consciously decide that you will be honest and live by strong moral principles. Once you have made that decision, you must then force yourself to live by that decision and must never allow yourself to be deflected from it.

Every time you are tempted to tell a lie or do anything dishonest, you must stop and force yourself not to do it. You must make a habit of acting honestly. Depending on how you have lived your life, this may prove to be easier said than done. However, by consistently stopping and correcting yourself, regardless of how small the transgression may be, you will strengthen your integrity muscle and in time you will develop the habit of being honest, come what may.

It's the same process with every strength, attribute and trait that you must acquire or strengthen. It's a process of mind over matter.

Suppose you also need to acquire or strengthen your positivity. First consciously decide that you will be positive and every time you think or encounter negativity, abolish it from your mind, by putting a positive spin on whatever it may be. In doing so, you will strengthen your positivity muscle. You will become a highly positive person. It's all in the mind. You must exercise control over your mind. It just takes time to master and achieve.

The formula for achieving mind control is:
1. Identify all those mindset obstacles that are preventing you from achieving your particular goal or target.

12: Acquiring Your Sufficient Winner's Mindset

2. Understand precisely what they are in order to know precisely what you must overcome. In this regard, it helps to precisely define each mindset obstacle in writing.
3. Identify and precisely define all the mindset strengths, attributes and traits that you must acquire or strengthen in order to overcome each particular mindset obstacle.
4. Consciously decide that you will acquire and strengthen each of those particular strengths, attributes and traits that are required.
5. Act on your decision and force yourself to abide by it. Make a habit of doing so. Keep practicing. Every time you find yourself succumbing to a weakness and not doing what you must do to achieve or strengthen the corresponding strength, attribute or weakness, correct yourself. Consciously force yourself to do what must be done and do it immediately. It will strengthen your resolve and in time will become a habit.
6. Make the same decision and follow the same process, one at a time, in order to acquire or strengthen each strength, attribute and trait that you require.
7. Do not wait to fully acquire or strengthen a particular strength, attribute or trait before following the same process to acquire or strengthen the next one. Repeat the same process for each of the other strengths, attributes and traits that you must acquire or strengthen. Depending on what you require you could soon be undertaking the same process to acquire or strengthen several of them at the same time.
8. In time you will acquire all the strengths, attributes and traits to the required degree and will possess a sufficient winner's mindset. Always remember your weaknesses and keep this process going to ensure you maintain the required strengths, attributes and traits necessary to overcome them.

Each time you attain a primary goal, set your next one by using the methodology explained. When you do, the elements of what constitutes a sufficient mindset may change. Be aware and adjust what's needed as necessary.

Other aspects

Ensure you are physically and mentally fit and stay that way. If you are, you will perform more efficiently and effectively. No one knows you better than you know yourself. Both mentally and physically, you will know if you are fit and healthy or if you are unwell or not at your peak.

Remember to make a periodic appointment with your doctor and undergo whatever medical examinations are necessary to ensure that you are not suffering from any condition that is likely to adversely affect your mental or physical good health.

If, at any time, you feel ill or not at your best, make an appointment with your medical practitioner and have your condition checked.

Stay fit. Regularly walk, run, swim, dance, exercise at home or at a gym or undertake whatever fitness program suits you.

Schedule and take regular breaks and make them part of your work schedule. Learn to relax. Try to leave work at work. Make time for family and friends. Get a good night's sleep of at least eight hours every night or during the day if you work nights.

Stay properly nourished and hydrated. Eat healthy meals and drink plenty of water.

Do not smoke. Do not take drugs other than as prescribed by a medical practitioner. If you drink alcohol, do so in moderation, however the occasional party where you let your hair down may help you unwind, unless there is a medical or other reason that prohibits or makes it inadvisable in your case.

Stay calm. Avoid stress. De-stress whenever you feel stressed or feel that your stress is building up.

In conclusion

Identify the mindset strengths, attributes and traits that you must have or must strengthen in order to attain a sufficient winner's mindset. Once you identify them, make a decision to acquire or strengthen those required to the requisite degree and follow through on your decision.

In acquiring or strengthening them, the formula is to force yourself to do what must be done and to never let yourself be diverted from doing so, whether by someone else or by your own weakness.

Know what you must do. Know why you must do it.

Always remember that only you are able to acquire a sufficient winner's mindset. No one can do it for you.

This book shows you what to do but, in the final analysis, you and you alone can acquire a sufficient winner's mindset for yourself. There is no other way.

So, don't procrastinate!

Just do it!

DIVISION 3
SELF ANALYSES AND REALITY CHECKS

13
YOUR SELF ANALYSES

Fundamental Principle Thirteen
Identify in writing those strengths, attributes and positive traits that you possess and the degree to which you possess them and those that you do not by undertaking a self-analysis.

In this chapter there are four sets of questions. The first relate to your essential strengths, the second to your driving strengths, the third to your supportive strengths and the fourth to your leadership attributes and pleasant personality traits.

When you have completed your answers you will have completed a self-analysis of which of those strengths, attributes and traits that you believe you possess and the degree to which you possess them. As a result you will be in a position to identify those that you do no possess and those that you possess to a limited degree and that need strengthening.

Your guidelines

Your guidelines for answering each of the four sets of self-analysis questions contained in this Chapter under Appendices 1 to 4 inclusive are as follows:

1. In the following four Appendices you are asked to answer the questions set out in:
    a) Appendix 1 in relation to essential strengths;
    b) Appendix 2 in relation to driving strengths;
    c) Appendix 3 in relation to supportive strengths; and
    d) Appendix 4 in relation to leadership attributes and personality traits.
2. When answering the self-analysis questions in each Appendix, first think carefully about each strength, attribute or trait, as the case may be, and honestly assess whether, in your opinion, you possess that particular strength, attribute or trait to any degree. If you consider that you possess the particular strength, attribute or trait to any degree whatsoever, answer "Yes". If not, answer "No".
3. If you consider that you possess the particular strength, attribute or trait, then on a scale of 1 to 10, with 10 being the highest score, rate the level at which you believe that you possess it, by inserting the appropriate number from 1 to 10 that you consider applies to you, as your answer. If you consider that you do not possess the particular strength, attribute or trait then your answer should be zero.
4. Answer each question separately. Repeat the process for each question. Do not proceed to the next question until you have completed each question in the order asked.
5. Upon completion, make a copy of each of the appendices containing the written answers to each of your four sets of self-analyses questions and file them in your folder entitled "Achieving My Primary Goal".

6. If in the future you acquire any of the strengths, attributes or traits that you lacked or strengthen those you possess to a sufficient degree, adjust your self-analysis answers in the above folder in order to bring your position up to date.
7. Your self-analysis records kept in the folder will serve as a reminder of those strengths, attributes and traits that, in your opinion, you possess, the degree to which you possess them, those you do not possess, those you must or should acquire and those that require strengthening.

APPENDIX 1
Self-analysis of essential strengths

This Appendix contains a series of questions to enable you to ascertain which of the essential strengths you possess, the degree to which you possess them and which of them that you do not possess.

No.	Question	Answer
1.	Do I possess "desire" as an essential strength to any extent? Answer "Yes" or "No".	
2	To what degree on the scale of 0 to 10 do I consider that I possess "desire" as an essential strength?	
3.	Do I possess "determination" as an essential strength to any extent? Answer "Yes" or "No".	
4.	To what degree on the scale of 0 to 10 do I consider that I possess "determination" as an essential strength?	
5.	Do I possess "passion" as an essential strength to any extent? Answer "Yes" or "No".	
6.	To what degree on the scale of 0 to 10 do I consider that I possess "passion" as an essential strength?	

7.	Do I possess "positivity" as an essential strength to any extent? Answer "Yes" or "No".	
8.	To what degree on the scale of 0 to 10 do I consider that I possess "positivity" as an essential strength?	
9.	Do I possess "focus" as an essential strength to any extent? Answer "Yes" or "No".	
10.	To what degree on the scale of 0 to 10 do I consider that I possess "focus" as an essential strength?	
11.	Do I possess "persistence" as an essential strength to any extent? Answer "Yes" or "No".	
12.	To what degree on the scale of 0 to 10 do I consider that I possess "persistence" as an essential strength?	
13.	Do I possess "commitment" as an essential strength to any extent? Answer "Yes" or "No".	
14.	To what degree on the scale of 0 to 10 do I consider that I possess "commitment" as an essential strength?	
15.	Do I possess "decisiveness" as an essential strength to any extent? Answer "Yes" or "No".	
16.	To what degree on the scale of 0 to 10 do I consider that I possess "decisiveness" as an essential strength?	

APPENDIX 2
Self-analysis of driving strengths

This Appendix contains a series of questions to enable you to ascertain which of the driving strengths that you possess, the degree to which you possess them and which of them you do not possess.

No.	Question	Answer
1.	Do I possess "drive" as a driving strength to any extent? Answer "Yes" or "No".	
2	To what degree on the scale of 0 to 10 do I consider that I possess "drive" as a driving strength?	
3.	Do I possess "proactivity" as a driving strength to any extent? Answer "Yes" or "No".	
4.	To what degree on the scale of 0 to 10 do I consider that I possess "proactivity" as a driving strength?	
5.	Do I possess "motivation" as a driving strength to any extent? Answer "Yes" or "No".	
6.	To what degree on the scale of 0 to 10 do I consider that I possess "motivation" as a driving strength?	
7.	Do I possess "ambition" as a driving strength to any extent? Answer "Yes" or "No".	
8.	To what degree on the scale of 0 to 10 do I consider that I possess "ambition" as a driving strength?	
9.	Do I possess "willpower" as a driving strength to any extent? Answer "Yes" or "No".	
10.	To what degree on the scale of 0 to 10 do I consider that I possess "willpower" as a driving strength?	
11.	Do I possess "creativity" as a driving strength to any extent? Answer "Yes" or "No".	
12.	To what degree on the scale of 0 to 10 do I consider that I possess "creativity" as a driving strength?	
13.	Do I possess "intuition" as a driving strength to any extent? Answer "Yes" or "No".	
14.	To what degree on the scale of 0 to 10 do I consider that I possess "intuition" as a driving strength?	
15.	Do I possess "curiosity" as a driving strength to any extent? Answer "Yes" or "No".	
16.	To what degree on the scale of 0 to 10 do I consider that I possess "curiosity" as a driving strength?	

APPENDIX 3
Self-analysis of supportive strengths

This Appendix contains a series of questions to enable you to ascertain which of the supportive strengths you possess, the degree to which you possess them and which of them you do not possess.

No.	Question	Answer
1.	Do I possess "integrity" as a supportive strength to any extent? Answer "Yes" or "No".	
2	To what degree on the scale of 0 to 10 do I consider that I possess "integrity" as a supportive strength?	
3.	Do I possess "reliability" as a supportive strength to any extent? Answer "Yes" or "No".	
4.	To what degree on the scale of 0 to 10 do I consider that I possess "reliability" as a supportive strength?	
5.	Do I possess "balance" as a supportive strength to any extent? Answer "Yes" or "No".	
6.	To what degree on the scale of 0 to 10 do I consider that I possess "balance" as a supportive strength?	
7.	Do I possess "confidence" as a supportive strength to any extent? Answer "Yes" or "No".	
8.	To what degree on the scale of 0 to 10 do I consider that I possess "confidence" as a supportive strength?	
9.	Do I possess "optimism" as a supportive strength to any extent? Answer "Yes" or "No".	
10.	To what degree on the scale of 0 to 10 do I consider that I possess "optimism" as a supportive strength?	
11.	Do I possess "enthusiasm" as a supportive strength to any extent? Answer "Yes" or "No".	

12.	To what degree on the scale of 0 to 10 do I consider that I possess "enthusiasm" as a supportive strength?	
13.	Do I possess "self-reliance" as a supportive strength to any extent? Answer "Yes" or "No".	
14.	To what degree on the scale of 0 to 10 do I consider that I possess "self-reliance" as a supportive strength?	
15.	Do I possess "adaptability" as a supportive strength to any extent? Answer "Yes" or "No".	
16.	To what degree on the scale of 0 to 10 do I consider that I possess "adaptability" as a supportive strength?	

APPENDIX 4
Self-analysis of leadership attributes and personality traits

This Appendix contains a series of questions divided into two parts to enable you to ascertain which of the leadership attributes and which of the positive personality traits you possess, the degree to which you possess them and which of them you do not possess.

Part 1: Leadership Attributes		
No.	Question	Answer
1.	Do I possess "leadership attributes" to any extent? Answer "Yes" or "No".	
2	To what degree on the scale of 0 to 10 do I consider that I possess "leadership attributes"?	
3.	Do I possess "the capacity for hard work" to any extent? Answer "Yes" or "No".	
4.	To what degree on the scale of 0 to 10 do I consider that I possess "the capacity for hard work"?	

No.	Question	Answer
5.	Do I possess "good communicationl skills" to any extent? Answer "Yes" or "No".	
6.	To what degree on the scale of 0 to 10 do I consider that I possess "good communicationl skills"?	
7.	Do I possess the capacity for "organisational skills" to any extent? Answer "Yes" or "No".	
8.	To what degree on the scale of 0 to 10 do I consider that I possess the capacity for "organisational skills"?	
9.	Do I possess "intelligence" to any extent? Answer "Yes" or "No".	
10	To what degree on the scale of 0 to 10 do I consider that I possess "intelligence"?	
Part 2: Personality Traits		
No.	**Question**	**Answer**
11.	Do I possess a "pleasant personality" to any extent? Answer "Yes" or "No".	
12.	To what degree on the scale of 0 to 10 do I consider that I possess a "pleasant personality"?	
13.	Do I possess "tcct" to any extent? Answer "Yes" or "No".	
14.	To what degree on the scale of 0 to 10 do I consider that I possess "tact"?	
15.	Do I possess "tolerance" to any extent? Answer "Yes" or "No".	
16.	To what degree on the scale of 0 to 10 do I consider that I possess "tolerance"?	
17.	Do I possess a "good sense of humour" to any extent? Answer "Yes" or "No".	
18.	To what degree on the scale of 0 to 10 do I consider that I possess c "good sense of humour"?	

In conclusion

Remember, that your answers to the questions in this chapter constitute your opinion. For that reason, in the next chapter, you are asked to have someone who is close to you and knows you well, independently answer the same questions in relation to you.

You will then be in a position to compare that person's answers as a reality check against your answers.

A reality check helps ascertain if you have been over critical about yourself when answering the self-analysis questions. It also helps discover any tendency on your part towards self-delusion.

14
YOUR REALITY CHECKS

Fundamental Principle Fourteen
As a reality check of your self analyses answers, have another person identify in writing what he or she considers to be your strengths, attributes and positive traits, the degree to which you possess them and those that you do not possess.

In this chapter there are the same four sets of questions relating to the same strengths, attributes and traits.

When you have had the answers completed by a close family member or friend who knows you well, you will be in a position to compare that persons answers with the answers you gave to your self-analysis questions. The comparison will act as a reality check and enable you to reassess the accuracy of your self-analysis answers.

Your guidelines

Your guidelines for having another person answer each of the four sets of reality check questions contained in this Chapter under Appendices 1A to 4A inclusive are as follows:

1. In the following four Appendices you are asked to have another person answer the questions set out in:
   a) Appendix 1A in relation to essential strengths;
   b) Appendix 2A in relation to driving strengths;
   c) Appendix 3A in relation to supportive strengths; and
   d) Appendix 4A in relation to leadership attributes and personality traits.
2. Select a person from your family or your group of friends who you believe knows you well and is capable of answering the questions contained in the four sets of reality checks in this chapter in an informed unbiased manner, such as to provide you a fair and honest assessment of the strengths, attributes and traits which, in his or her opinion, you possess, the degree to which you possess them and which of them you do not possess. Ensure the person reads and understands what must be done in order to complete the four sets of reality check questions. Select the person carefully. An independent, objective and correct assessment is necessary and will be most helpful in assisting you.
3. You must not show the person doing the reality checks, any of the answers you have given in your self-analyses. In addition, you must not say anything that may influence the person's answers to the reality check questions. However, you should show the person this chapter and ask him or her to read it as often as necessary and to fully understand what is required before answering any questions.
4. You should be present at all times during the process in order to answer any questions that the person may have and to provide

14: Your Reality Checks

whatever relevant information is needed provided you do so in a manner that does not influence or be likely to influence that person's answers.

5. Before the person commences to answer each question, you should ask that person to first think carefully about each of the applicable strengths, attributes and traits and honestly assess whether, in his or her opinion, you possess the particular strength, attribute or trait specified in the question. If the person considers that you possess a particular strength, attribute or trait (to any degree whatsoever), the answer should be "Yes". If not, the answer should be "No".

6. If the person considers that you possess the particular strength, attribute or trait, then on a scale of 1 to 10, with 10 being the highest score, the person should rate the level at which he or she believes that you possess it, by inserting the appropriate number from 1 to 10 that he or she considers applies to you, as the answer. If the person considers that you do not possess the particular strength, attribute or trait then the answer should be zero.

7. The person should answer each question separately and repeat the process for each question and should not proceed to the next question until completing each question in the order asked.

8. Upon completion, you should make a copy of each of the appendices containing the person's written answers to each of the four sets of reality checks and file them in your folder entitled "Achieving My Primary Goal".

9. If in the future you acquire any of the strengths, attributes or traits, you may ask the person (or another person who meets the criteria, if for any reason the first person is unavailable) to undertake a reality check for you on those particular strengths, attributes or traits that you consider you have acquired.

10. Your reality check records kept in the folder together with any updated records will serve as a reminder of those strengths, attributes and traits that, in the other person's opinion, you possess, the degree to which you possess them and those that you do not possess.
11. Compare each answer in the reality checks with each corresponding answer in your self-analyses and consider the difference, if any. If, as a result, you consider that a reality check answer may be valid and you make any changes to a self-analysis answer, you should adjust your self-analysis answer to reflect the changes made. Update your relevant folder as necessary.

APPENDIX 1A
Reality check of essential strengths

This Appendix contains a series of questions to be answered by the person you choose in order to ascertain that person's opinion of which essential strengths you possess, the degree to which you possess them and which you do not possess.

No.	Question	Answer
1.	Does he/she consider that you possess "desire" as an essential strength to any extent? Answer "Yes" or "No".	
2	To what degree on the scale of 0 to 10 does he/she consider that you possess "desire" as an essential strength?	
3.	Does he/she consider that you possess "determination" as an essential strength to any extent? Answer "Yes" or "No".	

14: Your Reality Checks

4.	To what degree on the scale of 0 to 10 does he/she consider that you possess "determination" as an essential strength?	
5.	Does he/she consider that you possess "passion" as an essential strength to any extent? Answer "Yes" or "No".	
6.	To what degree on the scale of 0 to 10 does he/she consider that you possess "passion" as an essential strength?	
7.	Does he/she consider that you possess "positivity" as an essential strength to any extent? Answer "Yes" or "No".	
8.	To what degree on the scale of 0 to 10 does he/she consider that you possess "positivity" as an essential strength?	
9.	Does he/she consider that you possess "focus" as an essential strength to any extent? Answer "Yes" or "No".	
10.	To what degree on the scale of 0 to 10 does he/she consider that you possess "focus" as an essential strength?	
11.	Does he/she consider that you possess "persistence" as an essential strength to any extent? Answer "Yes" or "No".	
12.	To what degree on the scale of 0 to 10 does he/she consider that you possess "persistence" as an essential strength?	
13.	Does he/she consider that you possess "commitment" as an essential strength to any extent? Answer "Yes" or "No".	
14.	To what degree on the scale of 0 to 10 does he/she consider that you possess "commitment" as an essential strength?	
15.	Does he/she consider that you possess "decisiveness" as an essential strength to any extent? Answer "Yes" or "No".	

No.	Question	Answer
16.	To what degree on the scale of 0 to 10 does he/she consider that you possess "decisiveness" as an essential strength?	

APPENDIX 2A
Reality check of driving strengths

This Appendix contains a series of questions to be answered by the person you choose, in order to ascertain that person's opinion of which driving strengths you possess, the degree to which you possess them and which you do not possess.

No.	Question	Answer
1.	Does he/she consider that you possess "drive" as a driving strength to any extent? Answer "Yes" or "No".	
2	To what degree on the scale of 0 to 10 does he/she consider that you possess "drive" as a driving strength?	
3.	Does he/she consider that you possess "proactivity" as a driving strength to any extent? Answer "Yes" or "No".	
4.	To what degree on the scale of 0 to 10 does he/she consider that you possess "proactivity" as a driving strength?	
5.	Does he/she consider that you possess "motivation" as a driving strength to any extent? Answer "Yes" or "No".	
6.	To what degree on the scale of 0 to 10 does he/she consider that you possess "motivation" as a driving strength?	
7.	Does he/she consider that you possess "ambition" as a driving strength to any extent? Answer "Yes" or "No".	

14: Your Reality Checks

8.	To what degree on the scale of 0 to 10 does he/she consider that you possess "ambition" as a driving strength?	
9.	Does he/she consider that you possess "willpower" as a driving strength to any extent? Answer "Yes" or "No".	
10.	To what degree on the scale of 0 to 10 does he/she consider that you possess "willpower" as a driving strength?	
11.	Does he/she consider that you possess "creativity" as a driving strength to any extent? Answer "Yes" or "No".	
12.	To what degree on the scale of 0 to 10 does he/she consider that you possess "creativity" as a driving strength?	
13.	Does he/she consider that you possess "intuition" as a driving strength to any extent? Answer "Yes" or "No".	
14.	To what degree on the scale of 0 to 10 does he/she consider that you possess "intuition" as a driving strength?	
15.	Does he/she consider that you possess "curiosity" as a driving strength to any extent? Answer "Yes" or "No".	
16.	To what degree on the scale of 0 to 10 does he/she consider that you possess "curiosity" as a driving strength?	

APPENDIX 3A
Reality check of supportive strengths

This Appendix contains a series of questions to be answered by the person you choose, in order to ascertain that person's opinion of which supportive strengths you possess, the degree to which you possess them and which you do not possess.

No.	Question	Answer
1.	Does he/she consider that you possess "integrity" as a supportive strength to any extent? Answer "Yes" or "No".	
2	To what degree on the scale of 0 to 10 does he/she consider that you possess "integrity" as a supportive strength?	
3.	Does he/she consider that you possess "reliability" as a supportive strength to any extent? Answer "Yes" or "No".	
4.	To what degree on the scale of 0 to 10 does he/she consider that you possess "reliability" as a supportive strength?	
5.	Does he/she consider that you possess "balance" as a supportive strength to any extent? Answer "Yes" or "No".	
6.	To what degree on the scale of 0 to 10 does he/she consider that you possess "balance" as a supportive strength?	
7.	Does he/she consider that you possess "confidence" as a supportive strength to any extent? Answer "Yes" or "No".	
8.	To what degree on the scale of 0 to 10 does he/she consider that you possess "confidence" as a supportive strength?	

9.	Does he/she consider that you possess "optimism" as a supportive strength to any extent? Answer "Yes" or "No".	
10.	To what degree on the scale of 0 to 10 does he/she consider that you possess "optimism" as a supportive strength?	
11.	Does he/she consider that you possess "enthusiasm" as a supportive strength to any extent? Answer "Yes" or "No".	
12.	To what degree on the scale of 0 to 10 does he/she consider that you possess "enthusiasm"" as a supportive strength?	
13.	Does he/she consider that you possess "self reliance" as a supportive strength to any extent? Answer "Yes" or "No".	
14.	To what degree on the scale of 0 to 10 does he/she consider that you possess "self reliance" as a supportive strength?	
15.	Does he/she consider that you possess "adaptability" as a supportive strength to any extent? Answer "Yes" or "No".	
16.	To what degree on the scale of 0 to 10 does he/she consider that you possess "adaptability" as a supportive strength?	

APPENDIX 4A
Reality check of leadership attributes and personality traits

This Appendix contains a series of questions to be answered by the person you choose, in order to ascertain that person's opinion of which leadership attributes and positive personality traits you possess, the degree to which you possess them and which you do not possess.

Part 1: Leadership Attributes		
No.	Question	Answer
1.	Does he/she consider that you possess "leadership attributes" to any extent? Answer "Yes" or "No".	
2	To what degree on the scale of 0 to 10 does he/she consider that you possess "leadership attributes"?	
3.	Does he/she consider that you possess "the capacity for hard work" to any extent? Answer "Yes" or "No".	
4.	To what degree on the scale of 0 to 10 does he/she consider that you possess "the capacity for hard work" as a strength?	
5.	Does he/she consider that you possess "good communication skills" to any extent? Answer "Yes" or "No".	
6.	To what degree on the scale of 0 to 10 does he/she consider that you possess "good communication skills"?	
7.	Does he/she consider that you possess a capacity for "good organisational skills" to any extent? Answer "Yes" or "No".	

No.	Question	Answer
8.	To what degree on the scale of 0 to 10 does he/she consider that you possess the capacity for "good organisational skills"?	
9.	Does he/she consider that you possess intelligence" to any extent? Answer "Yes" or "No".	
10.	To what degree on the scale of 0 to 10 does he/she consider that you possess "intelligence"?	
Part 2: Personality Traits		
No.	Question	Answer
11.	Does he/she consider that you possess a "pleasant personality" to any extent? Answer "Yes" or "No".	
12.	To what degree on the scale of 0 to 10 does he/she consider that you possess a "pleasant personality"?	
13.	Does he/she consider that you possess "tact" to any extent? Answer "Yes" or "No".	
14.	To what degree on the scale of 0 to 10 does he/she consider that you possess "tact"	
15.	Does he/she consider that you possess "tolerance" to any extent? Answer "Yes" or "No".	
16.	To what degree on the scale of 0 to 10 does he/she consider that you possess "tolerance"?	
17.	Does he/she consider that you possess a "good sense of humour" to any extent? Answer "Yes" or "No".	
18.	To what degree on the scale of 0 to 10 does he/she consider that you possess a "good sense of humour"?	

In conclusion

You have now had another person answer all the questions contained in Appendices 1A to 4A inclusive and in doing so, you have had the reality checks of all your self-analysis answers completed.

Carefully compare each reality check answer with your corresponding self-analysis answer. If, as a result of that comparison, you consider that you should alter your initial self-analysis answer for that question, then do so.

File your adjusted self-analysis answers in your folder entitled "Achieving My Primary Goal".

You are now ready to commence acquiring a sufficient winner's mindset. Do so methodically and step-by-step.

IN FINAL CONCLUSION

Be absolutely positive in your attitude at all times. Whatever we humans are able to conceive, we are able to achieve. It may take time, but given time, nothing is impossible.

Remember the story of the person who learnt how to fly in a wing suit and dived off a cliff to soar across the landscape and land safely in a paddock below. Before the flying suit was invented, such a feat was thought to be impossible. In reality, it was not. It was only a matter of time before someone invented a flying suit and it immediately became possible.

And so it is with everything. Given scientific, medical and other progress, it's only a matter of time before everything, whether physical or mental, will be possible. It's only a matter of discovering the knowledge that makes it possible.

Today a person may be bed ridden due to physical illness. In the future, with a transplant, that person could climb Mount Everest. Today a person could be suffering a mental illness or incapacity. In the future, with a transplant, that person could function normally.

Computer knowledge has already reached the stage where computer intelligence can exceed human intelligence. Today a person's brain capacity may be limited. In the future, with the aid of a computer implant a person's intelligence could be incredibly boosted.

Scientists have conceived time travel. In the future, time travel will be possible. It's only a matter of time before we will be capable of visiting other galaxies whether by time travel or some other means.

If the necessary scientific, medical or other knowledge does not occur in your lifetime, it's only a matter of time before it occurs for use by a future human generation.

You are capable of achieving whatever goal in life, career, business or any other pursuit within the limits of human knowledge that you set yourself to achieve.

You are certainly capable of being a successful person in life, career and business. The knowledge you require for that purpose is available now and is summarised as a formula in this book.

Determine your purpose. Know precisely what you wish to accomplish and never give up until you succeed!

Just do it!

www.ingramcontent.com/pod-product-compliance
Lightning Source LLC
Chambersburg PA
CBHW021404290426
44108CB00010B/381